THE CLIMB

Geraldine Doogue AO is a renowned Australian journalist and broadcaster, host of Radio National's *Saturday Extra* and ABC Television's *Compass*. She has won two Penguin Awards for excellence in broadcasting from the Television Society of Australia and a United Nations Media Peace Prize.

theclimb.org.au

GERALDINE DOOGUE

The Climb

Conversations with Australian women in power

TEXT PUBLISHING MELBOURNE AUSTRALIA

Photographs reproduced with permission: Ann Sherry, courtesy of Carnival Australia; Wendy McCarthy, courtesy of Wendy McCarthy; Heather Ridout, courtesy of the Reserve Bank of Australia; Alannah MacTiernan, courtesy of the office of Alannah MacTiernan; Sandra Levy, courtesy of the Australian Film Television and Radio School; Sue Morphet, courtesy of Sue Morphet; Gai Waterhouse, photo by Scott Barbour/Getty Images; Nancy Milne, courtesy of Australand Property Group; Sandra Harding, courtesy of James Cook University; Julie Bishop, courtesy of the Department of Foreign Affairs and Trade website – www.dfat.gov.au; Hilda Scott, courtesy of Hilda Scott; Christine Jenkins, courtesy of Christine Jenkins; Priscilla Collins, courtesy of Priscilla Collins; Simone Wilkie, © Commonwealth of Australia, Department of Defence.

textpublishing.com.au

The Text Publishing Company
Swann House
22 William Street
Melbourne Victoria 3000
Australia

First published in Australia by The Text Publishing Company, 2014
Reprinted 2014
This edition published 2015

Cover design by Text
Page design and typesetting by Imogen Stubbs

Printed and bound in Australia by Griffin Press, an Accredited ISO AS/NZS 14001:2004 Environmental Management System printer

National Library of Australia Cataloguing-in-Publication entry:
Author: Doogue, Geraldine, 1947–
Title: The climb: conversations with Australian women in power / by Geraldine Doogue
ISBN: 9781925240672 (paperback)
ISBN: 9781925095302 (ebook)
Subjects: Women executives—Australia
Leadership in women—Australia
Sex role in the work environment—Australia
Stereotypes (Social psychology)
Women—Australia—Social conditions
Dewey Number: 658.40994

This book is printed on paper certified against the Forest Stewardship Council® Standards. Griffin Press holds FSC chain-of-custody certification SGS-COC-005088. FSC promotes environmentally responsible, socially beneficial and economically viable management of the world's forests.

For my children and their families, and in memory of
Ian, whose influence so permeates our lives

CONTENTS

‘I myself will take up arms, I myself will be your general, judge and rewarder of every one of your virtues in the field. We shall shortly have a famous victory over those enemies of my God, of my kingdom and of my people.’

Queen Elizabeth I,
Speech to the troops at Tilbury, August 1588

INTRODUCTION

IN 2009, during drinks at Sydney's ANZ stadium, ahead of one of the first AFL Pink games supporting breast cancer research, I found myself in conversation with Julia Gillard, then deputy prime minister. Her turbulent days lay ahead, including a challenge to her leader, Kevin Rudd, and eventually running a minority government as prime minister.

We were chatting about the challenges of participating in the 'big game'—of politics, not football. And she said something that I have never forgotten: 'At the end of the day, when I go home and pull up the drawbridge, I want to be able to *recognise* myself.' I didn't have a chance to ask any follow-up questions. But I assumed she meant the prioritising of a secure identity in the midst of a big career. And that is the glittering prize, in my view. So even before she chose to step up to the top job, she had grasped something important. For a woman, advancing up the chain of command poses a special challenge: the community she comes to lead may be ambivalent about having a woman in charge, yet she needs to command its respect. Gillard's comment indicated something else that matters a great deal too: she wanted to like who she was becoming in this exercise of power. For both men and women, considerable shifts in psychology are required to bridge the chasm between being a follower and being a leader.

It helps, obviously, to hear stories of people who've made this transition successfully. The trouble is there've been so few accounts from women. This book is an effort to redress the balance. I wanted to highlight some of Australia's female leaders and to honour their dramatic peaks and troughs—but not to be reverential. All fourteen women who agreed to be interviewed were ready to discuss the good, the bad and the indifferent times of their career climb, at work and at home. What were the shared patterns, if they existed at all? Where and when did they spot the initial spark of ambition? What was the catalyst for their rise? Did mentors matter? What big setbacks occurred? Were they ever tempted to give up? Had they endured big showdowns with colleagues? How did a private life intertwine with the public one? Did they develop any ruthlessness in order to cope? Were they prepared, for instance, to persist at work *even* if their home life was under pressure?

So whether it is horse-trainer Gai Waterhouse acknowledging 'it's my way or the highway'; or university leader Sandra Harding warning colleagues not to confuse her politeness with weakness; or the most senior woman in the army, Major-General Simone Wilkie, admitting that real maturity as a leader involves knowing which rules must be broken; or Julie Bishop revealing that anti-women prejudice at the Adelaide Bar almost forty years ago still angers her and drives her, all the stories offer wisdom—and surprises—about taking authority in various arenas of Australian life in the early twenty-first century. I was surprised that many of the women admitted they withdrew from showdown fights, mostly with male colleagues, of the sort that leave metaphorical blood on the floor. But I was not surprised by the toughness they had all developed, or by their big dreams. They may not have relished the word 'ambition', which still frightens a lot of women, but almost every one of these leaders wished to make a difference in their worlds, not merely to add extra lines to their CVs.

Until now, the default characteristics of an effective leadership style have mostly been assumed to be masculine. Despite the occasional Margaret Thatcher, Golda Meir or Christine Lagarde, far more men have become legends as leaders: Nelson Mandela, Winston Churchill, Abraham Lincoln, Franklin Roosevelt, Zhou Enlai, Lee Kuan Yew, Mahatma Ghandi, Robert Menzies, 'Nugget' Coombs, Bob Hawke, Paul Keating, Henry Parkes, John Monash. The list could go on and on.

I hope to see far more narratives of women in power, or on the cusp of it. I want to hear a female idiom enter the leadership conversation. I want to revel in stories that sound familiar to me and my young female relatives. So much leadership literature seems excessively geared to males and is often very American in focus, whereas most of the contemporary advice is to move away from 'the great man' model and to emphasise far more the notion of developing your team's talents. Even so, the underlying tone in the copious writing on the issue of leadership somehow does not often welcome me, a woman. This neglect is under-appreciated in all the hand wringing about lack of female advancement. The leadership stories that are lionised are often full of utopian ideals and stress a solitariness that I don't believe gels with women's experience. Some of the most perceptive writing comes from female researchers. They are adamant that becoming a leader involves a fundamental identity shift, first and foremost, insisting that overt affirmation is needed to give the woman the fortitude to step outside her comfort zone and experiment with unfamiliar behaviours.[1] This idea applies to both men and women, but is more necessary for women. As researcher Herminia Barry wrote in the *Australian Financial Review BOSS* in October 2013, 'Integrating leadership into one's core identity is particularly challenging for women, who must establish credibility in a culture that is deeply conflicted about whether, when and how they should exercise authority.'

I love the line of the late Katherine Graham, the doughty *Washington Post* proprietor: 'To love what you do and feel that it matters...how could anything be more fun?' Wendy McCarthy, the Sydney activist and one of my interview subjects, offered a piece of logic back in the 1980s that has never left me: 'I've always had a strong view, ever since I identified as a feminist, that it must be possible to be a feminist, have a good relationship with a man and be a parent. If you can't be all these things, it means that ninety per cent of women can't be feminists. If only ten per cent of women can be true feminists, there is no future in it. And I believe there is a lot of future in being a feminist. It's a whole new perception of the world.'[2]

The newest cohort of female soldiers in line for leadership in the armed forces tend to be partnered, with children, compared with almost the exact reverse in previous generations, chief of army, General David Morrison, told me at his Canberra headquarters. This is surely progress. Maybe there'd be more, far more, women in positions of power if they could identify more with acclaimed leaders' stories. I strongly sense that young women need to approve broadly of the senior women around them before they will strive themselves. They need to believe that they'll *like* themselves if success comes.

Of course, we did have Julia Gillard as a model for a short time. Whatever one's politics, she was a woman of acknowledged power with whom other women could compare and contrast themselves. We could imagine how she felt, or so we thought; though as the pressure grew on her as prime minister, who among us could contemplate the ordeal of managing minority government? Whether it infuriated, intrigued or bored us, I believe her prime ministership altered the population's most basic grasp of the office, of power itself and of whether a woman could wield it. Her demise also triggered incredibly visceral responses. Nothing about her time at the helm was straightforward. There are widely differing verdicts on her talents. But, at the same time, many Australian women, and men, feel strongly that Julia Gillard was subject to types of discourse and representation that would never have been dealt to a man. For some anti-Gillard warriors, she moved into a category where anything goes, with no need for remorse about tactics; she was merely fair game, and an awful spectacle played out before us, tantalising some but horrifying most women, I suspect. Among some men, her time in power seems to have activated a form of deep-seated warrior response, with distinct overtones of sexual arousal, like the ultimate form of sexual contest. I found it revolting, hardly an inducement for the average woman to enter public life in Australia.

Gillard's defeat, in June 2013, prompted a lot of deep thinking about whether outsiders, including women, could realistically gain and keep power in modern Australia. Ever since, womenhave speculated on when it might happen again. How much did Gillard contribute to her own downfall? Were the talents that got her to the top, including her killer instinct, among those that contributed to her decline in some perverse way? Many women don't feel they possess those particular skills and may not want them anyway. But does that rule them out of high office? We profoundly need women to dream of attaining precisely that. The ghosts of the Gillard experience quietly accompanied me throughout all the interviews, but I didn't want to dwell on them. I was keen to meet women who had gained legitimacy in their field and who were accustomed to power and influence. After all the demoralising gender politics, I wanted, I confess, to hear some good storytelling. And I was not disappointed.

These were my yardsticks for choosing the fourteen women:

- They had to be governing others, either directly or indirectly via board membership. That meant ruling out some wonderful artists and performers who, by and large, work as single operators. I wanted to emphasise the talent of being responsible for others, which for me is the real summit still to be climbed, rather than merely personal development.
- I wanted them to be active now.
- I sought a range of states and interests, from government to business to community life.
- They had to be candid about their acquisition of power.

The stories the women tell are incredibly rich. They prompt some deep reflection on what forms ambition in the first place, and then what encourages women to take risks and to cope with setbacks. They also keep themselves in their skin, that great line from King

Arthur to his queen, Guinevere, in the musical *Camelot*.

Several fascinating conclusions emerged for me:

- Aspiration starts young. These high-achieving women are heavily influenced by their families of origin. I began to wonder whether this matters more, proportionally, than all the later sophisticated intervention measures. To a surprising degree, women cited their fathers' involvement in their formation, mostly favourably but not always. Mothers were mentioned, but much less often—which was quite a surprise.
- The women's families of origin were almost all actively engaged in their communities. Almost to a woman, their memories were not of bland, tranquil, households; instead, they remembered homes full of opinions and boldness, where parents were accustomed to speaking their minds within their communities.
- Very few of the women were up for 'the big fight', the last-ditch tussle for power. When it came to the night before battle, the women most often pulled back and let the other man (not necessarily the 'better man') win. It was as if the battle seemed, suddenly, not worth the likely casualties.
- Many of the women, but certainly not all, had experienced mentoring or sponsoring, mostly from men, but occasionally from committed older women.
- Many of the women felt they could improve as public performers in spreading their message. They accepted the crucial requirement of leadership as the need to 'bring people along'. Though magnificent eloquence,

> like that marking some of the observable male greats—people like Barack Obama—was simply not top of mind for any of the women I met.

I also sought a set of views beyond those of the women to test broader community perceptions. Nine prominent men, each of whom I respect, accepted my invitation to offer their perspective on women as leaders—again, looking at the good, the bad and the indifferent. They are all good observers of public mood; they've experienced their own climbs and falls; and they would all prefer more diversity in senior ranks. Their observations and predictions are full of insight and are candid too. Some of them may fall into the 'brave minister' category, but they add an extra dimension to the discussion of female advancement. They are anxious that gender isn't assumed to be the only explanation for some setback, though they never underestimate it: a slightly tricky balancing act. Men's constructive criticism is rarely sought these days, because it is deemed too risky for them to publicly discuss such issues, which is a pity. They have a lot of experience to share.

An American manager, a woman, summed up what I think is non-negotiable, or should be, about the duties of leadership versus those of parenting. She told Ken Powell, from the US food company General Mills: 'I realise that I am one of several people who could be brand manager for Cheerios, but I am the only person who can be mother to my children.'[3] Telstra CEO David Thodey cites his ideal workplace as one where people can bring 'their authentic selves'. The more we hear authentic stories about female pathways to governing others, like those in the chapters ahead, the more young women will dare to dream. And I may yet experience another female prime minister while I still have the energy to vote.

CHAPTER 1

ANN SHERRY

The Natural

One of Australia's leading businesswomen, Ann Sherry AO initially trained as a radiographer but then retrained in economics and politics and moved into policy work for the federal Labor Government under prime minister Paul Keating. Her next career step was into the banking industry, taking senior positions here and in New Zealand. She now heads Carnival Australia, the biggest cruise-ship operator in the Australasian region.

SOME people seem preternaturally equipped for leadership. Whether male or female, they have always intrigued me. Is it in their DNA? Did they have especially attuned parents, who fostered exactly those qualities that later morphed into the ability to lead others? Did they reach some magic tipping point somewhere along their life journey, altering a course that flipped them from follower or observer into outright leader? Or was it a much more gradual, more organic process?

Ann Sherry fits the bill of natural leader more than most. Occupying executive-level positions in Australia since 1992, Ann is often described as a leader others would follow over broken glass, that classic test of leadership where teams forgive mistakes, even welcome hardship, for the sheer pleasure of being seduced to step out of their comfort zones. The giving of purpose to another is one of the key leadership qualities I have come to prize.

Ann is now CEO of Carnival Cruises' Australian arm and its first female head. Carnival is the world's largest cruising company, and Ann has been president of the famous subset P&O since 2007. She started the job the week that the coroner handed down her findings on the Dianne Brimble case—the ghastly tragedy of a woman looking for love and excitement during a short holiday who was appallingly used by a group of male passengers who left her drugged to die alone in a cabin.

I wondered at the time what had possessed Ann. Coming out of a successful stint in banking, at Westpac in Australia and in New Zealand and the Pacific, this dominant businesswoman was plunging, eyes wide open, into a completely different sector, and one that seemed to be a basket case at that. The industry's reputation had been trashed by the Brimble story. Across Australia, people were riveted by the tales of exploitation and callousness that emerged from the coroner's inquest. Who'd want to go near this shabby outfit? No matter the exotic locales on offer, the court details suggested an industry that took people's money, got them on board and then turned a blind eye when a lord-of-the-flies environment developed. It showed a scandalous disregard for vulnerable women.

Responses were visceral. A group of building workers near the court frequently brought flowers to Dianne's mother and sister who were attending the hearings, to offer small consolation and to prove that men were ashamed of the male behaviour on display. Why would Ann, with her unblemished record, seek to take this on? Even at its more functional level, there was nothing especially noble about the industry, there was no social justice involved, no particular new standards to be set. It supplied a leisure product, pure and simple.

But Ann saw it differently. She saw a challenge. She embraced the risk, a cardinal point in her character. 'I run a very risky business,' she told me. 'Anything can happen and everything does happen: from bad weather to people who decide that they're going to go on a holiday and commit suicide. We had swine flu, quite a few years ago now: someone came onto the ship sick and suddenly I've got the *Marie Celeste* sailing up and down the east coast of Australia. My view is if it can happen, it will happen, and so we've constantly got to be thinking about how we manage that. What do we do? What's the right thing to do? How do we get on the front foot?'

This most recent chapter in Ann's career began in 2007 when Carnival's chair, another female trailblazer Katie Lahey, now chief of the headhunter company Korn Ferry, ran into her one day at a function. Was she doing anything much? asked Katie. Ann had just arrived back in Sydney after five years in New Zealand in charge of Westpac's operations there. When she replied, 'Not much,' the invitation arrived: 'Why don't you consider taking on Carnival?' Six years on, the results are in: during that time cruising has grown about fifteen per cent per year. Up to twenty-one ships now cruise to and from Australia, and there are plans for more. Carnival Cruises is set for continued dominance of the leisure industry.

Ann has thrived. The skills and mindset that encouraged her to say yes when so many others would have run a mile really interest me. Some characteristics predispose Ann towards high functioning. She believes in stepping up to life. She loves work, is energetic and needs to defray that energy, by her own admission. Above all, she is available when things go wrong; she almost welcomes crises. She embraces problems in ways that leave me gasping. For I can honestly say I have never welcomed crises. I find them enervating and creativity-robbing. Maybe this cuts me out of modern leadership contention. Yet Ann presents crisis management as an outright gift.

It started from the moment her son Nick was born with Down syndrome. She was twenty-one. Sink or swim? No, that's the wrong expression. There must have been some feelings of drowning when that much awaited baby arrived, but I doubt Ann ever considered sinking. She and her soul-mate husband, Michael Hogan, surfing mates since childhood, started problem-solving on Nick's behalf. And she's been doing it ever since—it goes very deep indeed.

Ann is very comfortable in her skin, something that is immediately obvious. Her upbringing—rural Queensland, father and mother both pharmacists, the eldest of three girls—set her up well. She worked in the pharmacy where she sold cosmetics for Christmas presents from the age of thirteen or fourteen. The pharmacy was a public service too, part of the respected troika of doctors, chemists and dentists that provided vital products and services to the people of the town. Ann was proud of the family's competence and status. Nick's condition was not in the plan, though, and no more children followed. That level of risk-taking was deemed too much even for this plucky couple. They decided to fight for him, for the best life he could have. It set up a pattern of not accepting the status quo, which continued throughout Ann's work: in the UK securing jobs for prisoners post-gaol and as head of HR at Westpac where she established paid maternity leave, making Westpac the first bank in Australia to provide it.

While I'd love the buzz and applause that goes with securing these big social shifts, such change is always accompanied by pressures, sometimes huge, as well as the need for exceptional strategic and tactical skills. We reporters love praising the results when something works and hurling blame when someone fluffs the challenge, usually with far too little curiosity about how plans were waylaid. Being an agent of change inside institutions is seriously tough. How does Ann manage that pressure?

Ann: In terms of pressure, I'm quite sanguine about what matters and what doesn't, because I think you can be pressured about things that don't really matter that much. In a moment of heat in organisations, you can see things build and build and build, often because of people's anxiety. I just think, let's step back and reflect on whether it really matters this much: how important is it, and is there a way through it? I am actually quite calm. Ironically, I'm probably calmer in really pressured environments than I sometimes am over whether the council has taken my rubbish bin away.

In this environment, particularly when you're leading people, you've got a responsibility not to be the petrol on the flame. You've got a responsibility to help people think things through to get to a good outcome, and pressure and anxiety are often absolutely the wrong thing. I think you learn that from your domestic environments. The moment you really need to be calm is often the moment that you're completely lost in a haze of anger and you can't think clearly.

I'm actually quite good at thinking stuff through and getting everybody down off the—sometimes—down off the ledge. So what do we do, and how do we find a different way forward? Rather than banging your head against something. Why keep doing that?

Geraldine: Do you think you've learned that? Were you always like this?

Ann: I would have been much more bull-at-a-gate when I was younger. I think you learn it—it's a long game we end up all playing. After a while you realise that the game is longer than the incident you're looking to manage, and if you take a slightly longer-term view, you'll find that that moment may or may not matter ever again.

Even if, as Ann suggests, you learn the art of recognising peak pressure arriving at the doorstep, how do you serenely lay aside your pre-existing agenda? This is super difficult. The pressures of huge editorial days or weeks I can manage well enough. More than four decades of media work and blended-family challenges have bequeathed that skill to me. But my anxiety about how much I'm leaving undone is always insidiously running alongside. When can I restore my normal routine? What have I forgotten? Whose feelings have I hurt while prioritising what I thought couldn't be avoided at work? Just because I'm obsessed with meeting the daily deadline, do my friends and family need to be similarly bewitched? Such is the monologue that runs around in my head. But not, it seems, in Ann's, especially not when she faced the disaster in 2013 of a young couple who drowned after they went over the *Carnival Spirit* ship's rails: an almost unthinkable tragedy.

Ann: Some of that cool-headedness I learned from my years in government, through all sorts of things and with some people who were very good at being clear about how you manage public messaging. I think there is a skill there that I probably have learned over time, but also there's a focus that you need to have. When you've got something you've got to do that's fundamental to the whole business, but which also is so important personally for those families, you just have to clear your desk of everything else. Anything that was on that day is gone. You actually go into another space. You get out of your usual work environment and go into what we call the emergency ops room. Everyone's concentrating, sitting around the table and whiteboards. We're very clear about what we've got to do. There's a discipline regarding those things, and that serves us very well. And that environment served me well.

Geraldine: You don't worry about what you've left behind? Obviously that's crucial too.

Ann: Everything else that was on that day in fact could have been on the next day or the day after, everything. So in those circumstances you've just got to be focused on sorting the issue at hand, because if you allow yourself to get distracted, you stand at a press conference with a hundred things in your head, and you can't have a hundred things in your head. You've got to be focused on what you're saying about the issue at hand.

The reality of it was that we needed to be focused on doing our best to see if those kids were still alive, which we knew was unlikely, but still you've got to do your best to see if you can find them and, if you can't find them, to get the information that at least gives the parents some sense of closure. And you've got to deal with the police in a very straightforward way as well. They're very supportive of us; we've worked very closely with them, but those moments

> are fraught with tension. Then you've got the whole world sort of gingering up a whole lot of nonsense.

Now here's a question. Do I necessarily respect this capacity to junk the ordinary weekly diary and its duties with equanimity? I know I should. It is probably central to decent leadership in a crisis: clearing the decks and establishing explicit responsibilities. But what commitments get lost along the way, and what or who are deemed disposable? Power comes into it, of course. Who or what has sufficient power to reorder a CEO's diary? Who, in the aftermath, picks up the pieces and does the housekeeping? Does Ann end up devolving it all to people beneath her, who don't have the same option to clear their decks? Do they end up working longer to sort things out? Surely there is a risk of becoming cavalier about the rest of the team and their problems.

What was thought-provoking about Ann's response was her total confidence in the virtue of setting new priorities in response to crisis, personally and professionally. Indeed, one could say she lives and breathes her own version of the theories of acclaimed American management guru Peter Drucker—about good managers being those who predict the future by creating it first—combined with her credo of seeking to improve the world. She has big dreams about changing things for the better, which in her eyes means allowing the people within an organisation to work to their full potential. This quality of respect for others, she believes, is a critical asset for any organisation. She wouldn't stay working with senior colleagues who didn't agree. There are plenty of eloquent company mission statements articulating the people-first priority. But they often amount to merely nice sentiments, honoured in the breach. For Ann, it is central to her identity as a manager and as a woman.

Nevertheless, many of Ann Sherry's employees no doubt have far more modest expectations and motivations, to which they are entitled. So how does she bring them along with her, on this far more demanding path, which she determines amounts to a collective good? This has emerged as crucial in modern leadership: imagining big futures for your team, articulating them so that they raise the pulse of less-imaginative followers, and then, crucially, translating them into action. It has become Ann's Holy Grail. But I am not convinced that all of the venerable women rising through our public ranks are terribly good at it yet. Maybe this was one of Julia Gillard's shortcomings, which then predisposed her to a wider range of assaults.

Ann: There are three things for me. One is that I communicate all the time. Communication is always written about in the management literature, but hardly anybody actually does it. I have regular management gatherings and all-staff gatherings. I go onto the ships; I spend a lot of time speaking to the people who work in the organisation, because they are the face of the organisation to the world, not me. I am occasionally, but they are every day. I think communication is really important. I like doing it; I'm good at it, and I think it helps people understand why things happen. The second thing is people need context, and again in most organisations the thing that never really happens is that people explain why stuff is happening. I think context is really important.

Geraldine: Even if the context is frightening?

Ann: Yeah, it doesn't matter what it is. People make better judgments if they understand why things are happening around them. Some staff are on the phones, and they're all out socially talking to people; I need them to know why we do things. It was the same when the couple went off *Carnival Spirit.* I gathered everyone together internally, and I talked about how terrible it had been; I talked about all the things we'd done, what was to play out, so people knew what was going on. Otherwise, they fill the gaps themselves and they make it up, as do people outside the organisation. But it's much better if your internal people at least understand why you're doing what you're doing.

Geraldine: They have an explanation.

Ann: Also, the fundamentals of the business give people good context. So whenever I come back from a board meeting overseas I always gather people together and I talk about what went on and what the issues are and what we're grappling with in the business and what that means for us in Australia and so on, because I believe that most people make better decisions when armed with better information. I'm not the only decision-maker in the business, I've got hundreds of people making decisions every day so I want them to make good decisions. I did it in banking as well, and in fact people often challenged me—saying, you know that's market-sensitive information you're giving people.

I'm thinking, well, maybe it is, but I'm happy to say to people, this is market-sensitive information so none of you can trade shares. As long as they understand that, there's no problem. And it does mean they're making better judgment calls about the customers they're dealing with all the time.

The risk-aversion mentality is so prevalent, where everyone tells you why you shouldn't do things because this terrible thing may happen. If you're in this mode, you end up making judgments based on what may be a one-in-a-million chance rather than what you know has a one-in-ten chance of happening. But if you do it, all these good things are most likely to happen. It seems to me that, on balance, I'm always on the side of possibility.

Geraldine: Do you believe rhetoric needs to be applied? By the sound of you, you don't.

Ann: No, I'm very straight. I think there's a lot of hubris in business. Really, there's a lot of that, but that's not me. There's a lot of talk about—it's interesting this phraseology—authentic leadership and so on. Really, what is authentic leadership? It's actually being yourself. You don't have to study to have authentic leadership, you just have to strip away all the nonsense you've probably learned. So, again, I probably didn't have somebody I was looking up to who did all that palaver. It's just the way I am.

Ann believes, as I'm inclined to also, that a risk-aversion mentality is settling in within various parts of our community—in business, politics and elsewhere. Risk mitigation is becoming risk avoidance, which, in Ann's view, is not an ideal state. We could have gone on to discuss the changing discourse around risk *ad infinitum,* but I was also interested in how she'd managed the alpha males around her, during her brilliant career. The challenges of 'bringing people with you' and of managing alpha males remain the two outstanding clear and present dangers to females thriving, in my opinion.

Ann: I've met a lot. The interesting thing is that they're aggressive with other alpha males, more than they are with women. There is a very strange thing: I watch sportspeople chest bump and I think that's an alpha male trait—no woman would chest bump; it would hurt. It's a weird thing to do. I've often said to people who try it on me, there's no point in trying to bully me: my father was a bit of a bully so I grew up in an environment where I learned to manage bullies very early; and I've worked for some of the biggest bullies in the universe. So really there's no point in trying to bully me because it doesn't work. And, you see, of course they have no plan B. I'm quite good at defusing as well, because I don't like the head banging. I just don't think it's very productive, and it's usually about ego, not about outcome. People usually back away.

I don't see that I've got to win and someone's got to lose. It's not that sort of dichotomy I play to. People outside the organisation say they think I'm tough. That's not how I see myself, but it's obviously how I'm perceived. I sometimes think that's probably because I am always clear about what I want and I am outcomes-focused. I've often dealt with people and thought, what do they want? Because, in fact, they don't know what they want either; they just want to look better than you. I don't play that game. It's not about ego. If there's something I'm really keen to negotiate or get, then I will go for it. I'm tenacious. I keep going and going and going until ultimately I get what I think is the right outcome.

Naturally, it hasn't all been onwards and upwards even for this focused achiever. Every successful career boasts its potholes, or worse. The received wisdom is that your mistakes and missteps are vital ballast. That may be, but the ratio of successes to failures should be heavily weighted towards the former. The British novelist Somerset Maugham had a pithy summary about character formation that rings very true to me: success doesn't spoil people; repeated failure does. Choosing your battleground and your weapons matter enormously, as does having sufficient confidence to ask for help.

Ann: I remember the first time I presented, I could see people going, oh Christ, get over it or get on with it—and of course I was the only woman leading any of the pieces of the business, any of the businesses globally. So I did have that moment of thinking: Am I relevant? Is what I said boring? Is it because I'm female in a very male environment? Or is it something else? Often the best way to find out is to ask someone. So I said to one of my colleagues…

Geraldine: Male?

Ann: Yeah, he runs the business in the UK and was very supportive of me when I started. So I said to him, just tell me what you saw then.

And he said, well, your story is great, but your relevance at the moment is low. You've got to grow the business for people to pay attention to you. I said, is there a thing about me being female? He said, no, no, if anything that's an advantage because you're different from everybody else. And I thought, okay, I've got it now. He was very straightforward with me, and in fact he and I still support each other. We've got a new global CEO, who had worked here first. I rang David in the UK, and I said okay, what do you want to know? He had a long list of questions and I supplied some information. So you find people who you can talk to in the organisation.

Geraldine: How long ago was that meeting?

Ann: That was six years ago.

Geraldine: What a helpful person.

Ann: Fantastic, a great insight. I've learned that it's better to ask, because you often get caught up in the noises inside your own head: is it this, is it that? I have been caught out like that. When I worked at Westpac one of the previous chairmen I knew did not like me—he and I just couldn't get on. I'd struggled to find the way to develop a relationship. He was really rude to me in a board meeting in front of everyone, and I just took it, sucked it up. Then I went outside and, again, spoke to a couple of people.

I said, what would you have done then? And one of them said, I would have told him to fuck off, and I was like, well, that wouldn't have helped. That was the alpha male response. Somebody else said, why don't you take him out for a coffee and ask him what his issues are? I thought, actually, that's a pretty good idea—I might as well ask him directly because I was trying to do it through finesse and blah-blah-blah. So, in fact, I just went into his office one day and said to him, look, we're just—you know—we're like ships, passing in the night. I don't know whether it's what I'm doing, how I'm doing it, whether there's something more you want. Interestingly, he was quite frank. He said, look, I come from an environment where there are no women, so I'm not that comfortable confronting you because I'm not sure how to do it. I said, why would you think you'd do it differently because I'm female? He said, well, because the way I interact with women is different from the way I interact with men. So I said, okay, that will be a good insight for me, but, I said, I'm giving you permission to interact with me the same way, which was probably a good thing to say directly to him.

Geraldine: Did it make him less or more hostile?

Ann: Look, honestly, he'd never liked me, but it made him less hostile in public. I also said to him, I think you're a bully, and he said, well, that's the way I get things done, and I went, okay. I said, I'm sure there are other ways. He said, but I've spent a lifetime behaving like this and I'm not about to change. I thought, well, you're the chairman and I'm not, so probably I've got to learn to live with that. He wasn't going to change, but he did moderate his behaviour in the meetings. You could see he fundamentally didn't think women should be in these jobs, and there was just nothing I was ever going to do to shift a lifetime of belief.

Geraldine: No, but you stayed there?

Ann: Oh yeah, I stayed and he went. I knew he had his turn at the helm. I outlasted him, which was a victory, but a sort of a pyrrhic victory, because he didn't really change, though he wasn't rude to me in meetings any more.

Ann Sherry says she constantly looks five years ahead, to discern where Carnival should be, what the competition is doing, what her team needs to be doing now to get there ahead of them. She can relax over a DVD boxed set or with friends, but she isn't one to lie around in the sun. Oh no, that would be too passive for Ann. She is a big dreamer and a passionate social reformer, and she has combined these ideals with the organisational prowess and leadership capacities required to follow through on change programs. What's more, Ann seems to derive so much fun out of these ventures, more than many people at the top are prepared to admit to. Her energy is infectious. Her confidence in her ability to lead others is quite settled. The tag 'the natural' is very apt in her case.

CHAPTER 2

WENDY McCARTHY

A Woman's Place

Wendy McCarthy AO was a teacher to her bootstraps till she discovered community activism via women's liberation, the Women's Electoral Lobby and the Family Planning Association. She has held various positions on a mix of private and public boards, and her life has forever been marked by eclectic interests and passions. She chairs McGrath Real Estate, Circus Oz and sits on the boards of headspace NationalYouth Mental Health Foundation and Pacific Friends of the Global Fund. Until recently, she and her daughter Sophie worked together at McCarthy Mentoring, offering mentoring services to young women and men.

WENDY McCarthy has said yes to many invitations to lead organisations in the public and private sectors, including major entities that feature regularly in the financial press and not-for-profit start-ups: an unusually wide range of groups. Precious few fell within her comfort zone, but each time, she threw herself into the role completely. She exemplifies a style of leadership that combines the head and the heart, an operating principle that she is passionate about. She has taught herself to lead; she was probably not a natural. So her experiences of triumphs, setbacks, loyalty tests and pressured decisions are incredibly salutary. In her idealistic twenties and thirties she saw no need to learn traditional leadership skills to create the better world she wanted. Whereas now she believes the attainment of these skills is the true last frontier for female advancement. The naivete of her early years of activism now stuns her. Those years could have been full of rehearsal and practice, of smart observation about the world of power and influence, a time of learning exactly those skills she now tries to bequeath to her daughter's generation. Back in the early 1970s, armed with big dreams about creating new worlds, Wendy and her co-founders of the Women's Electoral Lobby felt that formal leadership was part of the very system of hierarchies and power games they wanted to leave behind. Their brave new world would have less status attached to office-holding and be more amenable to feminine negotiation, more community-based and, vitally, something fluid. 'It recognised leadership as a position on a continuum and that people could move from leader to follower and back again,' Wendy wrote in 2011.

How utopian that sounds to me now, with several decades of working life behind me, as it does to Wendy. Creating an appetite within the wider community for mature, female leadership preoccupies her these days. And she simply never stops honing her own skills and those of the women around her. She and her fellow activists once believed that if they could change the machinery of government regarding basic equity rights and education, change would be 'inevitable, incremental and linear': get enough women into positions of considerable power, support them especially from the top, change some laws and just wait. All will come right. As sure as night follows day, talent will out. That was the thinking.

Well, it did not happen like that. The reasons why not fascinate Wendy. Her conclusion is that cultural barriers were much more complex than she'd realised, particularly with regard to timing. Women invariably don't identify their ambitions till later in their professional lives, when children have been raised, sexual identity has settled and managing relationships is no longer such a high priority. Only then is the mastery and resilience required for mature leadership within reach, she believes. The trick then is to grasp the idea that your time might have come just when you may have ceased the search.

Wendy can be very blunt if you ask for advice, yet you know she is on your side. She loves seeing a woman striving to extend herself to combine public and private life: the glittering prize. But she won't pander to any whingeing about being a victim, and on more than one occasion she has virtually told me to 'get on with it'. What makes her advice useful is her privileging of what she considers non-negotiable elements of people's life cycles—coupling, building families, earning a living—which are all important and never to be denigrated in her eyes. Some mentors almost wish them away. Not Wendy. If anything, she is more convinced than ever that women who acknowledge these traditional arenas of life in their choices gain a credibility that is invaluable.

> Wendy: People who don't appear to recognise these fundamental stages of life or who don't acknowledge their importance are often punished severely. If we own them well, people are inclined to say she's a good family woman, and that plays to everyone; it's one of the things that brought Julia Gillard undone, I regret to say. Motherhood is an experience that she hadn't had, but it adds to your fullness. You are a much more rounded person when you've done those things [family, children], and I've come to the view that as women live seven years longer than men on average we have an extra seven years to get many of those things in place. So I would say to young women, just hang in, in some way. Don't disappear. Don't go away. If you have to, step back for a bit and do other things, but think of it as development and learning and nurturing of your soul.

I could never have imagined that I'd be doing the things I've done since I turned fifty-five. And there's no role model really. There's no script in my documentary! I'm making it up as I go. But I think, more and more, I can afford to take more risks because I'm more financially stable. My children's lives and reputations no longer hang on me. They all have a more important person in their lives for first reference than their father and me.

That's a job of parenting really well done, I think, and I'm very proud of that. But I can do other things for myself now, and I can take those composite skills into leadership positions, where I'm often meeting people who haven't had the security that you get from having achieved that. People who would cross the road because I was a feminist espousing stuff twenty years ago hire me to run their companies now. The same men. I don't want that to sound smart. We've just all grown up a bit. I haven't left the game. We have things in common now that we can share and solve together. My leadership style is calmer; it's better informed, and I have a huge understanding of how communities and people in them work—something that most men with linear careers have not the faintest idea about—and this knowledge is a consummate skill in every boardroom. Women who just follow a male career path don't have that either. My career has not been linear and incremental. It's been lateral and incremental and involved some high-risk decisions. I've learned how to manage risk. I'm not risk averse.

Most of Wendy's career decisions have been made with a degree of contained terror, even right back in her early days in the Family

Planning Association, where she began a pattern of changing the cultures she joined. At the time, it was all a bit 'penis-and-vagina-ish', as she puts it, because nurses were in charge and they were good at physiology and biology. Wendy wasn't. So she made a virtue of not being proficient at analysing plastic pelvic models, and she reframed the organisation's conversations. It was a long way from her first professional job, as a teacher. The classroom had felt like home to Wendy and she loved it. But the regulations of the time didn't love her new life as a freshly minted young mum, just back from a glorious three years in the UK with her husband, Gordon. All she was offered was possible casual work. So began her pattern of reinvention, starting with the decision to leave teaching and join Family Planning. Then came what seems now like an inevitable progression towards taking on more authority, not that it was nearly so clear-cut at the time. On two notable occasions, with heart in mouth, she accepted invitations to sit on boards.

In my experience, this opens up new worlds, of somewhat baroque manners and codes, which are probably unfamiliar to many men too but certainly to most women. If Wendy noticed them, she did not let them daunt her. One of the boards was that of the ABC. She was invited to join as deputy chair in 1983 by a Hawke government senior minister, the late Senator John Button. The other was the board of the Higher Education Authority, which she joined in 1980 at the invitation of charismatic and controversial New South Wales Labor minister, the late Paul Landa. He virtually bludgeoned her into it.

> Wendy: He rang me and said, I want you to go on this board. I said, I don't know anything about higher education. He said, have you got a university degree? And I said, yes.

Well, that's enough, he said. I said, I don't think so, and I think so and so would be better. He said, I'm asking you…you cause me grief. Everyone thinks you know everything about it. Do you want to be inside or not? I said, can I have until tomorrow to think about that? No, he said, you've got one hour. Anyway, I rang back and said, yep, I'll do it. That was life-changing for me. I learned then to say yes to opportunity and to work out how to do it later. When I went on that board, I was the only woman with seventeen men, and they all seemed to be engineers or bureaucrats from AWA [Australian Wireless Association, the pre-eminent industrial communications specialists of the time]. Honestly, they spoke in a foreign language. To start with I really didn't know anything, and then, after about a meeting and a half, I suddenly got it.

I learned a lot from that experience. If you're going to be the person who proposes a change issue [raising the training of nurses to university level], then you have to accept some responsibility for finding the solution. The solution involved showing my inadequacies and incompetencies and lack of knowledge by going into a place where I was seen as a lesser person and taking the punt that I could find my way through, which I did.

That board experience prepared her for the next, the coveted ABC position.

Wendy: I remember someone saying, what the hell would you know about broadcasting? I said, hmmm, don't know, really, not much. They said, well, should you get that job?

I've got it, I said, so I'll have to make the best of it. Years later I asked John Button why he invited me onto the ABC board. He said, because you could do social change. He said I could put a question into the community and help resolve it, that we had to change the ABC into something that was reflecting more of Australia. You could argue your case and you could take people with you, he said.

Wendy heard the same flattering verdict from others. One comment that she loves and which cemented her self-belief as a legitimate contributor came from the late senior ABC manager Stuart Revill, who was in charge of board liaison, when he was leaving the Corporation in 1992.

Wendy: You know, you've been a great addition to the ABC board, he told me during his farewell. So many people were fearful of you and of your reputation, he said. But what I've found is that you bring great clarity to the organisation. You paraphrase complexity in a way that makes it easy for people to understand. You make it clear what the job at hand is. That is a singular skill. From the point of view of people on the board, who seem to obfuscate rather than clarify, it is a great benefit. And you turn up, he said, to face the music.

She had turned up to face black bans on senior managers after her insistence on there being a woman on every single interviewing committee. Word spread around the ABC that Deputy Chair Wendy McCarthy took no prisoners, that if she detected implicit or explicit ambivalence about female advancement from managers she'd go for them. Dare I confess that, though thrilling, it worried me, a more timid soul, that she might provoke a backlash from the powerful men. Such was the predicament of young, emerging female workers in big entities like the ABC with well-established cultures dominated by lionised men. We weren't even sure we had the right to think of ourselves as heirs to all this, let alone heirs on our own terms. What were our own terms, for that matter? That took me years as a journalist to work out. There is nothing overnight about any of this.

Eventually, on the subject of wielding influence and power, a vital metamorphosis occurred for Wendy: the transition from bravado to genuine poise. Even if it was brokered by clear-sighted men, the big shift for Wendy was internal and all her own work. She came to judge her capacity to cut through, to see the innards of a problem, as one of her central assets. This was a profound shift that didn't happen until the mid 1990s, twenty years after her first appointment. And with it came, oddly enough, the calmer leadership style she described earlier, as if she lowered her shoulders and relaxed into a higher quality of work.

These days, Wendy's various board commitments—Circus Oz, McGrath Real Estate, Pacific Friends of the Global Fund, headspace National Youth Mental Health Foundation, Goodstart Early Learning—are conducted in a much more under-the-radar style than her earlier positions, where she regularly hit the headlines. She is arguably more effective. Wendy aims to preside over board meetings that are fun, where people want to attend, where a sense of common purpose and engagement in something bigger than yourself trumps straight duty. She absolutely wants no micro-management part any longer— been there, done that, she says—though she enjoys enabling others. There must be some learning involved in everything she takes on, and she welcomes the rigour of the commercial profit motive, even though she is possibly best known for her not-for-profit work. Her reasons for accepting the chair of John McGrath's highly successful creation McGrath Real Estate are revealing.

Wendy: I might say to myself, people think real-estate businesspeople are lower than snake-oil salesmen. Yet the most profound decision young people make and the most significant financial decision in their lives is property— buying their first home or aspiring to. So if I can influence a business and help people to understand that, that matters. Why does McGrath work in the area of homelessness? Because we sell houses to rich people and the homeless are the mirror image. I always kind of look underneath, and I try to take that conviction with me. You know, John McGrath and I talked and I said, we must never lose sight of the higher order because that's what you need if you want good people to come, and we have a lot of very well educated people who work here because they can actually see a bit of a higher order as well as the money.

All Wendy's appointments involve political manoeuvring and wrangling complex boards. However, she's not drawn at all to the mainstream political arena. She had a taste of it very early in her career, in 1974, when she was persuaded to stand for North Sydney Council for the McMahons Point borough as part of a resident action group protesting against development. This is so often the classic route that transforms quiet, suburban mums into full-on activists. Not so for Wendy.

Wendy: I hated every single minute. Asking people to vote; I didn't want to ask anyone to vote for me. I loathed the

> whole thing. I thought, this is not me. Some people would say I'm a wuss because I didn't want to go to a vote, but others would think, well, she knows herself well enough to know what she's good at. I don't like the sense of being tied to a policy that I might completely disapprove of because I happen to be part of this group. It's not the way I operate best. So that was my blooding really. I thought, no, this is not for me. But can I compete? Yes, I think I compete in other ways, and I think that if I've done a good job, people will ask me to do other things. That's worked for me. There are two people at the moment asking me to go on boards, big boards.

The challenge of competing emerges as a significant part of the leadership quest for most of the women interviewed, as does the dedication required to maintain a leadership position. While not always demanding a 24/7 commitment, leadership roles certainly require it when crises hit. It is also presumed that a leader will prioritise and foster new relationships within their work communities. In some senses, this is reasonable, but for women who typically invest so much in relationships outside work, this mandatory work sociability presents an added challenge. Above all, it's assumed that modern corporate leaders will cultivate a repertoire of elite qualities: strength and suppleness, prudence, an ability to read a balance sheet effectively, good connections, or good-enough anyway, and a goodly cup of charm.

It's always a small shock to see how much time and energy Wendy still commits to her leadership roles. Dividing herself between her personal and professional duties has been tough at times over the years. Several big tests were thrown up by her earlier experiences at the Australian Bicentennial Authority, where she worked between 1986 and 1988. She joined as one of three general managers. I remember her excitement at the prospect of stepping up to this big job that was so important to Australia. But within a couple of weeks, another general manager had joined in a very similar job to hers. What's more, Wendy didn't seem to have a budget.

Wendy: I'd always remembered Gloria Steinem saying that you only count when you know what your budget is. So I went to the CEO and said, well, where's my budget? No, don't worry about that, he said. I had that moment of sickening dread. Actually I haven't been hired, I thought, because I'm cute, competent and extremely good. I've been hired as a bit of a name and a token woman because they're in trouble here.

It was so humiliating, and I was the deputy chair of the ABC at the same time. I thought, they don't even like me. Well, I thought, it's a bit hard to go away now, so I started competing. I got a budget, but in some ways I didn't realise quite what I was doing. I remember thinking, okay, so there was a general manager of marketing, and of programs, of admin and finance, and then a woman came in as general manager of community affairs, which I thought was my job. So I was given general manager of communications. Anyway, within a year I had by far the biggest portfolio. I had competed! And one of the blokes said to me, nice run-through there—basically you've taken most of our jobs. I remember thinking, did I do that deliberately? And I thought, no, I don't think I set out to do that. I just set out to get myself a proper job in that organisation. In between time, of course,

> the CEO was sacked, the chairman was sacked; another chair came in, our third in three weeks, and he said, Bob Hawke is coming to visit us on such-and-such a day, two days hence, and I want everyone at their desk. I want the prime minister to see that this place is really organised. I said, well I'm actually not going to be here that day. He said, you are, you're the only one who knows what goes on here. I said, I'm actually not because I have a two-year standing commitment. My husband is opening a state-of-the-art factory in the western suburbs. John Button, who's leader of the senate, is coming to open it. I cannot change it. I have my children going to it. This is the biggest thing in my husband's life, and, just in case you don't know, he's done this while he's had leukaemia, and I'm going, and that's all there is to it! Well, he said, you'll lose your job. That's fine, I replied. That night I get a phone call from one of the cabinet ministers to say, what do you mean that you're not going to be there when the PM goes? Do you think you'll ever get another fucking job from the Labor Party? I can tell you now if you think that you can go to your husband's factory opening—I said, state-of-the-art factory, western suburbs, employs people, you know, people like forklift drivers. Do you know any? Gordon does! This man goes on, you'll never get another job, Wendy. I'm trying to protect you. I said, well, bah!

So Senator Button, the respected industry minister, duly arrived by helicopter, the factory opening went well, and Wendy did not lose her job. But she did not escape scot-free. An article mysteriously appeared very soon after on the front page of the *Sydney Morning Herald*, alleging that Ms McCarthy was 'double-dipping', in being paid by the ABC and the Bicentennial Authority. Fortunately, Wendy had sought an official opinion from the attorney-general before taking the ABA job. But the *Sydney Morning Herald* piece led to a phone call from Prime Minister Bob Hawke, saying the resulting controversy meant she had to choose which job she wanted to keep.

> Wendy: Well then, I'll choose the ABC, I said. He said, no, you're needed at the Authority. I said, no, because the ABC's my heart. ABA could be, but it's not as important. Anyway, then the communications minister, Michael Duffy, produced the legal opinion I'd sought earlier and got in writing. Then, six months later, when I finally met Hawke, he said, oh, you're the person who prefers her husband to me! Isn't that classic? I said, that's right. Out of that, I have to say, I really learned about holding my ground—I'm just not going to be bullied by alpha males. Yes, they are capable of giving me what they think is a gift [a board or executive position], but it's actually a task. The fact that I choose to embrace it doesn't mean that it's so important to me that I'll throw away the rest of my life. I won't. I think that to be a rounded leader, you need to have had a few scarifying moments like that to know really not only what you stand for but also how much you will put up with. I think it's profoundly important to know how much you will take.

This led us back into the territory of alpha males and competing and issues of ruthlessness. Wendy's other, more recent, story is sobering too—a reminder that rising to the top or near-top means that the waters are not safe, that you are breathing rare air, that others covet your position. What might be asked of you, in order to remain or move further up, when a threat emerges?

Wendy was knocking on the door of wearing a big 'first woman' hat. She was excited. For the last seven years, she had sat on the international board of Plan International, the seventy-five-year-old international development organisation that works to lift children out of poverty. The chair's position, based in Denmark, was becoming vacant. Wendy thought she had the undivided support of a particular colleague as a sponsor. Other women in the organisation supported her standing too. But she suddenly realised that her assumed sponsor was cultivating someone else in what was becoming quite a murky little contest. It forced some serious reflection.

> Wendy: I thought, hmmm, this is going to actually be quite ugly, or quite intense. So I went away, went right back into myself and said, how much do I want this? Do I want it because I want to be the first woman or because of what can I bring to it? And what are the disadvantages? And the person who might get the job, I actually thought would do a good job. It's just that it wasn't a woman. I thought, I need to get over myself. I don't think this is necessarily the right time for me to do this job, and I don't want to be away from Australia for maybe two months or six weeks at a time. I didn't want to live like that. That consideration has informed all my leadership positions and roles in my life. I think I'm brutally honest with myself. As it happened, the bloke being touted as an alternative candidate came to me and said, some people are asking me to run against you—I don't actually want to run against you. Because if you really wanted it,

> I would come with you as the deputy. I said, no, you're a world banker, you have four languages, you're retired and you have three pensions. I still need to earn a living, I have one language and I'm far away. So why don't you and I agree? And that's how it played out.

Accordingly, this late-arriving candidate, a man, got the job. Some of Wendy's female supporters were really cross with the process. Importantly, Wendy didn't feel she'd surrendered. 'I just labelled it differently!' she said. She 'cut a deal', but by making the decision not to compete or join in the game-playing, she did lose, which had its searing elements for her even though she describes it dispassionately now. Subsequently, another woman, an experienced Danish diplomat, has just proudly taken up the role as first female head of Plan.

The game plays and what the McKinsey Group called 'the envisioning skills' required for leadership are two aspects of Wendy's repertoire that we both agreed were works-in-progress for many talented women. We had both digested the fascinating details from INSEAD's huge study of 12,000 women, completed in 2007 and updated in 2013.[4] It highlighted eleven specific leadership qualities, mostly shared by both genders, though women had the edge in several categories, especially in the close development of their team. The broad categories included people development, role modelling, offering appropriate expectations and rewards, communicating efficiently, being inspirational. But there were two where women were not pre-eminent: in the critical area of envisioning, the ability to recognise new opportunities and trends and to develop a new strategic direction for an enterprise; and in cut-through, disruptive leadership, being prepared to break established rules if the situation demanded it, which could be transformational in encouraging workers to perform beyond expectations. Women, say the researchers, tend towards more transactional leadership, where they prioritise daily exchanges with their team to achieve agreed performance targets. In other words, less spontaneous, less improvised, on-the-run decision-making, but more steady.

> Wendy: I think I'm guilty of not envisioning enough. I don't go out like the heroic general or the male warrior who's seen as the archetypal leader, saying this is where we're all going and this is how it's going to be; let everyone know what they're up for. I tend to stay with the group and say, let's all go together. But I'm going to start doing that a bit this year. You have to find your voice to envisage. You probably need to be the CEO or the chair to be able to do that.

At the famous end of the day, however, searing personal challenge has shaped Wendy's career choices more, possibly, than anything else. Her husband of fifty years, Gordon, was diagnosed with leukaemia in 1981, throwing the entire family into unprecedented turmoil. His treatment—bone-marrow transplants, total isolation for the sake of his immune system, chemotherapy—was relentless and wearing. Thankfully, he was cured, with a bone marrow transplant in 1988, and, speaking of reinvention, turned himself from a businessman into a prize pedigree-cattle producer, moving to farmland in country New South Wales in the early 1990s. But the whole experience was Wendy's dark night of the soul and nothing, absolutely nothing, in life since then competes with those terrors. Naturally, the experience provides unrivalled perspective.

Wendy: I learned to live every day as it comes then, because that's how we had to live. I decided I didn't want to waste time; I wanted to be sure that every day was as good as it could be. It sounds so corny when I say it. The first year, when I was still sort of paralysed, he'd get a bad cell count or something and I'd be playing the funeral in my head. Then I'd think, smarten yourself up. I did things that got such public disapproval, like going back to work. People felt the need to take me aside and say, you should stay home and look after your husband. That would be the worst thing I could do, I'd say. I would make him sick, and he doesn't want to stay home, he wants to do stuff.

But I did learn that sense of living in a Buddhist way: for the moment and of the moment. I've tried to get the kids to understand that too, and that's how you do it; that's when you take your opportunities, and that's when you look after the things that you care about.

Amen to that.

Amen to the idea, exemplified by Wendy McCarthy, that this business of leading is not linear. It certainly takes courage but, for her, it is driven by a clear set of values and a healthy ego. They have enabled her to spar with some of the more established players, some of the 'bulls in the paddock'. She has learned to trust herself in big tussles that require chutzpah as well as deft strategic judgment. She has even enjoyed it, despite the occasional wild ride involved. She has even learned to join the big players' teams when invited. The truth is she has had the time of her life.

CHAPTER 3

HEATHER RIDOUT

The Influential Girl Next Door

Heather Ridout AO grew up in country New South Wales, but left for the University of Sydney in 1974 to study economics. This led to a career representing Australian secondary industry, first with the Metal Trades Industry Association as a researcher officer, and then eventually as the leader of its successor, the Australian Industry Group. Over the past thirty years, Heather has become one of the nation's main commentators on manufacturing, training and wages policies and has contributed to a range of related government inquiries. She is now a prominent member of senior boards, including the Reserve Bank and AustralianSuper.

IN some ways Heather Ridout is a poster child for leadership qualities developed through basic good rearing. One of twin girls born to Bill and Goldie Ridout, in Deniliquin in southern New South Wales, she enjoyed not merely an idyllic childhood, but also one full of purpose. Her parents created an engaged household, adopting their very own 'life: be in it' ethic. Her memories sound like a textbook guide for forming well-rounded, sure-footed adults. Her parents were competent, with clearly articulated values, and were completely committed to their girls and the village beyond, yet they had a modesty, even a humility, about their own talents. They represented a very Australian middle-class sensibility of the mid twentieth century with their quiet but deep ambition. For young Heather, the yield was unambiguous treasure—a deep-seated confidence about her place in the world, whatever postcode she chose, whatever vocation.

Yet, at the same time, Deniliquin was always there for her, should her good run in the city dry up. Could she step back, whenever she liked? Probably not. Well and truly a city girl now and long accustomed to having her phone calls returned by the heavy-hitters in the CBDs and in Canberra's power circles, Heather possesses serious influence. She sat comfortably on several significant government reviews simultaneously during the Rudd-government era. She is attuned to these rarified climes without compromising her Aussie girl-next-doorness—there is always that sense that she could knock out a batch of playdough to occupy the kids just as easily as analyse the next balance sheet. She plays this considerable asset to advantage, without artifice: she displays rare congruence between a classic image of ever-present motherliness and clear strategic focus. Her whole idiom, including the colloquialisms she uses, makes Australians feel at ease. She manifestly loves the high-level influence peddling and policy formation, yet she doesn't take it too seriously, or so it seems. When *Sun-Herald* writer Susan Chenery published an article on her in 'Sunday Life' in May 2009, it included a jarring assessment from one highly placed source: 'A "fragrant little woman" she ain't. She is steely minded. There is a sizeable ego as well.' Heather mightn't even argue with this. But hers is an ego that chooses its fights carefully.

Under Heather's parents' ideals, people should grow to their full potential. It was a simply a waste not to, though they showed absolutely no sign of harbouring aspirations for their girl to achieve what she did by 2012: a position at one of *the* seats of Australian power, the Reserve Bank board. This would have stunned Goldie, but shocked Bill, who, for all his devotion, did not really believe in educating girls, according to Heather. Over the years, he most certainly came to change his mind on that score, but it wasn't instantaneous. Politics and the community always mattered in the family, as did volunteering and participating. For the Ridouts, the ABC was essential, delivering details about their region and the world beyond, day after day. It offered regular connections between her safe little territory and others that might beckon. In this environment, without her even realising it, Heather's confidence continued to grow, and she developed the adaptive skills she has needed to tackle the challenges offered her. Considerable grit accrued as well, despite her self-described tendency to worry—about not doing enough and not doing well enough to meet the task at hand. Her family life in Deniliquin and then her time at boarding school may have formed her, but her rise to power and influence has meant capitalising on some more recently acquired skills.

Geraldine: Did you experience people disappointing your good will, exploiting it?

Heather: I don't look back that much. I know at the time [of starting at the Australian Industry Group], I had some pretty rough times, but I tend to always look forward and I forget about it. I mean I can't even think of the worst thing that ever happened to me. I can't remember. Actually I think it is a bit of a defence mechanism. You do say, oh well, it's time. 'F-One-Eleven' is one of my favourite expressions. Shoom! [With a sweep of her hand upwards like a plane taking off.] I'm not a dweller on that sort of thing, but I am a dweller in that if I don't do something very well, I'll put myself on the rack.

I'm quite hard on myself. I always have been but I don't dwell on other people. I mean I'm disappointed when people fall short in those sorts of ways. But I tend to get more disappointed that I underestimated them.

Geraldine: Have you had to sack people?

Heather: Yes, I have. It's very, very difficult. I find it hard, whatever the circumstances. Making people redundant is a shocking thing. There is no easy way to do it. You just have to be very straight and honest. You know, even if people are really badly behaved and damage the company, it's still pretty awful.

Like several women who've risen to positions of power, Heather benefitted from working within a stable organisation over a long period, in the ambit of an increasingly influential figure who believed in her, despite her own misgivings. For her, it was the legendary Bert Evans, the veteran head of the Motor Traders Industry Association (MTIA), which morphed into the Australian Industry Group (AI Group). He was one of those old-style quietly effective lobbyists, in the days when manufacturing industries commanded much the same attention as the Business Council of Australia does now. Bert dominated his field and everyone knew it. I met him several times during my on-the-road reporting years, and I liked and respected him. I remember watching him, this ideas man, subtly coaching Heather, as he did others on his team, conferring an effortless reassurance that their opinion was valuable.

When Heather was recruited by him to be MTIA's new industrial officer in 1977, he must have known she'd need to assimilate into a very masculine culture. An early model for the peak bodies that now dot our corporate landscape, MITA represented the heavily unionised metal trades manufacturing sector. So this fairly protected young woman, with an economics degree and a new husband, took a big gulp and, with her father's advice to 'just throw yourself in' ringing in her ears, agreed to join. Despite the foreign territory, she encountered courtesy from her male colleagues, mostly. Not everyone was amenable, especially as Heather was gaining kudos as one to watch. And there was her lack of confidence to manage. Her first AI Group boss was 'indeed tough, a very demanding taskmaster and I think that was very destructive for my confidence.' But fortunately for Heather, she had years to mature within the organisation, and over the next three decades she adapted to different external and internal challenges. Meanwhile, the ambitious Bert simply wouldn't accept her insecurities. He kept giving her more and more to do, increasing her duties in line with the organisation's growing significance. He planned to make her a director. She didn't have to guess how some of her colleagues felt—half of them made it clear they didn't want her in that role. Eventually she was made an executive officer, the highest rank below director. And, importantly, she finally accepted that Bert's confidence in her was warranted. This was probably Heather's crucial crossing of the Rubicon, though another more important paradigm shift came via children, exactly as it had for me after my daughter Eliza was born in 1983. I felt 5000 feet tall, ecstatic about the achievement of giving birth, more poised than ever before in my life. What *couldn't* I take on? The feeling didn't last, but that sense of unique new purpose marked the end of one life and the start of another, profoundly.

Heather: I think it made me feel a more complete person, and I do think having the children was so incredibly important. It was very good for me. At one stage, I had three children under four, and even though that was hard—I had one with colic and Peter [her husband] was working hard—I loved it. I remember the day they all were sick: one came home from school at lunch, one woke up in the morning with chicken pox and then the baby got it, so I said, I'm taking a week off work. And they're all there together and I went up to the video shop and I said, stay in the car because you're all covered in spots! And we had a party for a week, the kids and me; we were a real little unit. So they always had Mum. We had great times together.

Geraldine: Did it round you out?

Heather: It gave me a better understanding of people. I think those mothering instincts bring out qualities in you that, as a boss, you are the better for. I think I was a nicer boss, more understanding, more interested in the people working with me.

How often I have noticed this result for women. Yet I've rarely read about it in the management literature. So maybe this is important to acknowledge. It takes some time to grasp *how* you have been rounded out. First-time mothers are invariably overwhelmed at the start, seriously doubting whether their personal life will ever be the same again, let alone their professional life. Then you realise incontrovertibly that it won't be the same, and somehow things clear. It might sound melodramatic but, in some sense, there is a death-and-resurrection aspect to it. Many old assumptions about what can be reasonably asked of one woman are junked. They are simply not fit for purpose. So you yield to the 'new normal', realise that your whole notion of time management has to shift, and you devise clever, sometimes ingenious, solutions that had never dawned on you previously. The baby demands so much attention, it forces much more carefully planned goal-setting on the new mother. Can I hope to make that coffee date with friends today or in two days time? Can I fit in that hair cut this week? Can I write that short column, which needs a bit of research, or is that a ridiculous aspiration? When the baby goes to sleep, can I trust that I'll have the energy to join the conference call that my colleagues have thoughtfully scheduled to fit in with my breast-feeding needs, or will I be too exhausted to do anything but fall asleep? However prosaic, the end result for the mother is much cleverer planning, better predictive abilities about the time needed to achieve things, and less perfectionism. The inevitable crises created by the baby's change of routines as it grows and develops force even more adaptation. Just as you accommodate their little ways, after great discernment, the little dictators change the rules! And so it goes throughout that first twelve or so roller-coaster months. Adapt or die Mum, is the subtext from the baby, and indeed many women (and, as we're increasingly learning, a lot of new fathers) struggle mightily with the reinvention required. But, I suggest, all these challenges are perfect rehearsals for higher-level work and decision-making. At home during my daughter's early life, I consciously mined my working life to remember how I coped with all manner of newspaper and television challenges. Surely one little human bundle could be 'learned' and 'mastered' too? It helped that I was in love with the child, of course. But in the noisy hurly-burly of babies and household management, critical skills acquisition creeps up on mothers without fanfare. You learn to chip away at the task at hand, rather than to aim for the sky—such a vital lesson in being a good enough mother as well as a manager. Your identity subtly shifts, you come to terms with growth, feel more of an all-rounder, because you are. The emotions tapped by motherhood receive good, regular workouts along with the weariness of the so-called double shift. But they also engender the precise type of fitness required for the modern workforce. I doubt this has been fully recognised as the advantage it is. Might acknowledging this extra armoury of skills conferred by motherhood help a transition to greater authority outside the home? The 'mummy track' could even become a drawcard. Heather certainly believes that good careers are not linear, that they 'go in all directions, influenced by all sorts of people', indespensible advice she received from Bert and others at the AI Group, which she passes on to young women whenever she gets the chance.

> Heather: I set very high standards [at the AI Group]. We had to be the best! The boss, the CEO, basically has three tasks. You have to set the direction, set the standards and put the right people in the right places. Do all that and you're in business. It sounds much simpler than it is, but I think having the children and having that balance in my life made me a better boss, and it made me really drive a very positive culture that was very much about individuals being supported by each other. We had a very tight team: we put in place some terrific people. They all loved it because they were really capable. And we had to be energetic. I was always wanting to do something new. What about this? What about that? I have always been an ideas person. It was interesting and so I started to get going, and I say to the kids now, if you don't like the job, get out of it, but if you're in a job that doesn't work, find the ten per cent or fifteen per cent you really like and prise it open. That's what I did. I found this spot and I prised it open and created a whole role for myself.

The decision to take on the chief executive role was, in itself, a small saga involving some instinct and some grit. It contains some real lessons. Heather had advanced, under Bert's guidance, to being director of public policy. It was a big, lively job, with influence and full of interaction with journalists and good thinkers. Heather was happy and satisfied. By now, the mid 1990s, Bert had retired and been replaced by well-known industry representative Bob Herbert, who had been an MTIA director. Then Bob flagged his retirement in 2008, meaning the main, much-desired job would soon become available. But Heather, and others, thought that someone was already marked out for it, a man whom she respected. She didn't even think she'd be considered, and, as it turned out, another big job in a similar organisation loomed into view. Bob advised her that if she was considering it, she'd need to let him know. She had moved to that rarified level where she had to consciously put herself forward to be selected. After some inner turbulence and serious thinking at the last moment, she went to his office and came out with it: the other organisation wanted her to be chief executive. It proved to be decisive.

> Heather: Bob said, what will it take you to stay? Initally I said, to be deputy director, which was in itself quite a move for me. It was only after I said that that I had this other turning point, this tilt at being CEO. I had an instinct, somehow—I still don't know why I actually made that call. I didn't want another $500,000. I wanted that position. I wanted to create the option for myself. Whether I took it was another thing. I thought, do I want to be CEO and take on all this responsibility for process and for managing three hundred people and buildings and councils, governance—all those fairly big things? And

> I wasn't sure I would be very good at it, because I tend to rely on other people to do a lot of that. But actually they were the best years I had. I was worried that members would resign but no one did, and I worried about staff turnover, again just a worry. But I had a terrible feeling. This other guy, who had been promised the main job—but I didn't know that—didn't speak to me. It was pretty unpleasant and he just left the organisation, though we're great friends now. But in the end, I was really amazed that we all worked so wonderfully well together. And when I left, grown men cried when I announced it, which overwhelmed me. I really feel that people did look to me. And some tough men, in a lot of areas, said, the golden years of my career were working with you as chief executive.

However, being CEO is a 24/7 vocation. This should act as a serious pause to many people with bubbling ambition. How many really wish to be on call throughout the day and the night, even if the requirement is accompanied by, sometimes, very big bucks? How many are happy to accept that they will be seen as an embodiment of the organisation, as a sort of custodian of others' hopes? The role doesn't offer much downtime, or that luscious retreat into a safer, private world. One of the interesting findings in my sojourn around leadership is the level of sociability required of the modern leader. Mostly, I met women who are fairly extroverted by nature to whom this may come easily. Some, just a couple, seem to be introverts who have learned to develop their convivial side. But all accepted the need to put on a show, to be the public face of the entity, to turn up, to give 'the speech'. Now there's a challenge for even the best-equipped leader. And the honest among the women acknowledge the small fun moments of life that are pushed to the side, which is a genuine loss.

Heather: You really don't get away from it. When I was chief executive of the AI Group, I lived and breathed the job. Wherever I went, people knew me because of that role, and they still do. I do think you epitomise the organisation. If you're actually a leader, if you really embody the values and the identity of the organisation, which I think the CEO should, you are really effective. But I think you also need balance in your life. I didn't have any option because I had three kids, so there was this automatic 'well, where are you, we need you, you have got to be here' from them. Actually, as a chief executive you do have a little more control over things: you can set the meeting times. And when I became chief, I stood up in front of the staff, all of them, and told them what I stood for. I said, I think you already know me. I've worked here for twenty years, but I just want you to know what I stand for. And one of those things, of course, was work and family, and I always said that work intrudes on the family you love so much, so family has a right to intrude on your work life. I introduced paid parental leave at the AI Group, which was the first thing I did. It created a wonderful culture.

Geraldine: What skills would you still like to learn?

Heather: I used to say to the staff every year at the Christmas party, I hope you've done something this year that you never thought you could do at the start of the year. I've always felt you've got to keep growing—that's where I envy children. They do so many things for the first time. It's like bungee jumping, but that's not me at all. I'm not an adventurer, I'm a built-environment girl these days. There are a lot of things I've lost that I'd like to get back. I used to play the piano and I loved it. I'd like to do it again. I used to play a good game of tennis. Things like that have gone because I just had to let them go. I wouldn't mind reacquainting myself with them.

In terms of work skills, probably giving a better speech. People say I give good speeches, but I tend to be...well maybe, maybe not. Maybe I've just come to accept the way I do things.

Being CEO generally means walking, fully exposed, into controversy at some point. Heather's had her fair share of such experiences, but possibly none involved the level of pressure of her decision in 2007 to reduce the AI Group's support for Prime Minister John Howard's Work Choices plans, a cornerstone of his government's policy and his political beliefs about less-regulated labour markets. Heather had initially supported the plans but changed her mind. So she walked right into the white-knuckle zone of political contest, Australian style. Ten years earlier she'd presented the MTIA's position on wages and training, alongside her then boss Bert Evans, to the Hawke–Keating cabinet. She knew this arena to the core. No neophyte when it came to political tactics, she knew absolutely how red hot this issue of distributing the nation's earnings between capital and labour was. So when Howard won his majority in both houses of parliament in 2004 and set out to implement his long-standing dream of deregulation, she could see what was coming. She was immensely torn, she says. She could see how other peak bodies were responding, and she didn't approve. The awful moment of truth was approaching for the AI Group.

Heather: I was rung up by Chris Uhlmann [chief political correspondent for ABC's influential *AM* program at the time], and I made my decision there and then, because I thought, if I vacillate, too many influences will come to bear on this decision. So I said, I'm not going to do it [agree with the prime minister]. That was an instinct. I would have resigned if I hadn't been able to take that stand. So would others in the organisation. It was a big call and I certainly went back and talked to councils [within the AI Group] and all sorts of people about it and they endorsed the decision. I took the brunt of it for the organisation and all the criticism came to me personally. It was personal. And it lingered. It probably lingers still.

Geraldine: A lot of it was very personal. It didn't seem to weigh on you though.

Heather: No, I felt better for it, because I couldn't have looked myself in the mirror. We had never advocated that policy. We gave John Howard eighty-five per cent of that policy, which was a terrific document, and he did these extreme things on the end of it, which were things that really undermined the whole integrity of it. I had felt that I was supporting it because I had to, because a lot of our members did want it. I used to go and do media interviews along these lines with people like Greg Combet on the TV. It was really hard, and I was getting so much abuse from people I respected. I lost friends because I was supporting this thing. I was getting no thanks, only criticism, and when the full policy document came out, I thought, enough's enough: I am going to do what I think is right. Our organisation had a 138-year history, and we had survived because we never messed with party politics.

Whether or not this could be seen as standing back from party politics is debatable. Heather's decision did get tossed around in the media. In that highly charged time, it was a significant sign that not all employers were necessarily in favour of the prime minister's plans. It mattered to the turn of events. So, Heather is no slouch when it comes to a fight. She seems unfazed about the number of alpha males that you're bound to meet in territory like hers. Neither does she seem to be overly bothered about the number of manoeuvrers who are found in and around politics. She forms her own strategic responses and is aware of theirs, but she doesn't seem to become obsessed with trying to second-guess every next step—a trap I have seen others fall into.

Heather: I've met quite a few alpha males and I take a dim view of them. You think to yourself, what's this guy all about? They can be very smart people, but they are challenging. I always try to figure out what they are like, and then often we become great friends. I've dealt with many, many of them, so they don't worry me. But I don't like cocky bastards. I like substantial people, and if you're just a competitive person who likes to compete because that's all there is, I can't bear it. I like people who engage, and I don't mind if they engage in an alpha-male way but I don't like them just reinforcing their own sense of self. It doesn't interest me. I tend to show lack of interest and walk away. I don't worry about it. I'm not going to let them get to me.

Geraldine: But you're not in awe of their powers, or their strength?

Heather: Not at all. They do have some strengths, there's no doubt about it. They do. Bill Kelty [ACTU secretary 1983–2000] was an alpha male, huge intellect, brutal tongue, and, you know, Keating, he was an alpha male, but I liked them because they were so interesting and capable.

Geraldine: What about being in a real fight? I've been trying to work out whether women resile from the big fight, and I've discovered that some very tough women do. Do they read the situation and say, that's going to be a bloody big fight and I'm not sure I'm up to it?

Heather: I've told people, a couple of alpha males, what I've thought of them, and we've ended up being very good friends. The way I look at a fight, I mean, I draw a line in the sand and say, look, we are going to have to work together so I will agree to disagree, but I'm not going to have any more to do with you than I have to. In the end, I think they've never been spoken to like that—and in one particular case we get on famously now.

Geraldine: What had he been doing?

Heather: He was just rude, obnoxious, throwing his weight around, that sort of thing.

Geraldine: Visibly or behind the scenes?

Heather: Visibly, in meetings and on social occasions. He just thought he could push me around. He wasn't working for

> the AI Group; he was an outsider. And he was just rude. It came to a head one evening when I was at a dinner, and I just thought, I'm not going to take this. And so I had a crack. I wouldn't take him on in front of other people, but he'd been rude to me in front of them. It was terrible. I was mortified, absolutely. But in the end, I realised you can't let it happen. Culture is the most important thing in organisations. People should think a lot about it. Its importance has been really reinforced in my career. Sometimes the male culture makes an assumption that women are weak, that we can be trodden on or that we don't fit into the competitive culture that men have created. But I think having women in organisations makes for a better culture; otherwise, you get a dominant-male culture, which is incredibly competitive.

In the latest *Australian Financial Review* Power Index, Heather Ridout came in at number nine (from unlisted the previous year) in the list of Australia's top ten covert powerbrokers, considering her positions as chair of the huge industry super fund Australian-Super and board member of the Reserve Bank and Australian Stock Exchange. 'A previous power lister when heading the business lobbyist Australian Industry Group and being close to the Labor government, Ridout is steadily evolving into a Gonski-like presence across business and broader policy,' said the Power Index summary. However, one of the panellists, prominent Sydney banking identity Mark Johnson, said, 'She's probably less powerful now than she was with AI Group, where she had a direct interface with policymakers and decision-makers. She's now in positions of higher elevation, but they're much more consensus-based roles.' Indeed, Heather says, along with better speech-making, her key goal now is to become a really good non-executive director: understanding how the entity works, asking the right questions, querying in the right way, being able to analyse material well. So, as ever, Heather is learning on the job, having a crack at it. Her father—the former president of Rotary, of Legacy and the local hospital board, who started the first nursing home in the Deniliquin area, who ran the picnic races each year—could never have imagined it. But his set of principles is the one she's using as a model, finessed to her very own creation. And I detect she is not nearly finished yet.

CHAPTER 4

ALANNAH MacTIERNAN

Crashing Through

Alannah MacTiernan started her working life with degrees in arts and law, and moved straight into Aboriginal employment and training work. Her public life began almost thirty years ago with her election to the Perth City Council, followed by her move to the Western Australian State Parliament, where she represented the Australian Labor Party. There she carved out a distinctive career as minister for planning and infrastructure from 2001 until 2008. Having decided to step out of politics, she changed her mind when the former federal Labor member Stephen Smith resigned his seat of Perth, which she subsequently won in the 2013 election. Alannah is now shadow parliamentary secretary for Western Australia.

ALANNAH MacTiernan's reputation precedes her these days, from her time as minister in charge of making the trains run and building things during the Gallop and Carpenter ALP governments in Western Australia (2001–08). Wherever you go in my home state, everyone knows Alannah. Everyone has a take on her. It is usually a pretty good one, and mostly bipartisan too, though such a big character inevitably provokes some disapproval. Plus there was that pesky business of her losing her licence no less than three times over almost two decades—for speeding, drunk driving and sundry points losses. A saint, she isn't. But overall, she is perceived as real, gutsy, out-there, genuine, a cut-through person despite, or maybe because of, her invariably messy appearance. She is one public woman who absolutely does not over-fuss about style. As a group of Pilbara women told me back in 2008, 'She comes striding out to meet you, the clothes don't necessarily match and the choices are, well, strange, but who cares? She's magnificent!

She's herself.' As herself, she fully grasped her power as minister for planning and infrastructure to transform public transport in Perth with the construction of a range of rail and road projects, especially the seventy-kilometre Mandurah Line that is a model of contemporary urban people moving. Many thousands of lives were transformed by the efficient travel link from outer-urban homes by the water to the city. The rail halved the drive time, providing Mandurah residents with a forty-eight-minute trip to jobs in the city—without which, many people would be stuck in low-income traps due to lack of local work. No wonder Alannah is proud of brokering this amenity. It surely amounts to the best type of labour reform: impressive in planning and delivery, and fulfilling working people's aspirations.

Alannah is an acknowledged, experienced leader, toughened in the cauldron of Western Australian ALP politics and now chancing her arm in Canberra. Although there are few Labor members in the west, she refuses to believe Western Australia has become a conservative enclave, beyond rescue for anything resembling progressive or Labor-focused beliefs. A good old-conviction politician—but don't take that to mean predictable or orthodox—she's known for being battle-scarred, for having a 'ballsy narrative', to quote one newspaper article. And even though she is entering her seventh decade, these days regarded as the 'evening' of a political career, she clearly has more to con-tribute. Knowing her record, I would definitely not write her off. She *will* contribute and make waves. And she could offer some surprises. I can speak from experience. I first met Alannah in June 2013, in the ABC's Perth studios, as part of a series of Radio National pre-election forums. Our event was arranged weeks before. But that day, out of the blue, the sitting ALP member for Perth, the respected Stephen Smith, dropped a bombshell: he announced he wouldn't contest the next election. Bruised and exhausted from years in the front line of the Gillard–Rudd battles, with Rudd back as prime minister and, at that early stage, looking like the successful comeback kid, Smith surrendered the precious seat he'd held for ten years. A young lawyer, Tim Hammond, had been working the area for a while, putting in the hard yards to secure ALP preselection whenever it came up in Perth. Alannah wasn't in the race. Although she now denies it, I saw the gleam in her eye as we fiddled with our drinks in the green room prior to that June forum. She was suddenly transformed by Smith's announcement. I could hear the barely suppressed adrenaline in her hastily organised drive-show radio interviews. I sensed that a fuse had been lit beneath her, her ambition renewed; her eyes focused on the big league that she'd coveted.

In the 2010 federal election, she'd fought very well in the seat of Canning and, against all odds, had nearly knocked off the sitting Liberal member Don Randall. Her consolation prize was to become mayor of the City of Vincent in the fast-growing northern suburbs of Perth. After, in her words, 'overwhelming pressure' to stand, and without ringing one person to ask for support, she put her hand up for Perth. All other contenders were swept aside. She campaigned as well as everyone expected she would and initially appeared to have increased Smith's majority. The final count, however, showed a 1.5 per cent swing against her. Still, a very creditable result, as the rest of Western Australia maintained its ferocious hostility to Labor. So how and why does she swim against the tide so effectively? What do her achievements tell me about community leadership?

For a woman like me, just one year older than Alannah,

brought up in the same Irish-Catholic tribe, she's a fascinating study. With an upbringing surrounded by the nuns, the local parish, music, horses, betting, politics and arguments, and with a strong mother, her early life resembles mine in so many ways. Except that she grew up in Heidleberg, in suburban Melbourne, and I in probably less political South Perth. Alannah says she stopped believing in God at the age of fifteen. But, to my eyes anyway, the faith deposit remains very strong indeed in Alannah, and it explains a lot. She reminds me of what many Australian Catholics seem to have lost: their membership of a working-class tribe with well-defined values, duties, loves and hates. It was full of security, even if only the security of knowing who you couldn't stand. And it bequeathed her something precious, which propels her forward like probably nothing else can: a sense of vocation, almost a calling to public life. Maybe, by tapping into something beyond mere ego, you are as well prepared as any SAS operative is for battle. And it all started with mother's milk.

Geraldine: When you were younger, did you imagine this was where you'd be in your life?

Alannah: At about eight or nine, I'd thought fleetingly about it. But, really, when I started to become politically active I didn't have in mind that I would be a member of parliament. I always knew that I was going to be really interested in politics. I've always had the view that you couldn't complain in a democracy. I guess I had worked out pretty early in life that if you want to affect things you've got to be involved, and that it actually is important to the nature of our society that people are involved in getting fairness, justice and good things happening in Australia.

Geraldine: Was that led by your parents?

Alannah: Well there was an element of that that I certainly got, obliquely, from my mother. She was a strong Labor supporter, though she felt the need to vote DLP, just to mollify the church, but always gave her preferences to Labor, until later when she felt free to just go straight to Labor. So it was, probably, my grandfather, who had been the sort of person who was very involved in absolutely everything in his community. I suppose in an osmotic way, you acquire that understanding.

Geraldine: Maybe it was the notion that the world belonged to those who turn up!

Alannah: I guess it was not so much that the world belongs to you. It was more than that: it was a sense of duty, that you had an obligation to participate.

Geraldine: Did the nuns at St Bernadette's give you that as well?

Alannah: Again, not overtly. But look, the other thing was that we did grow up in a Catholic parish that was very, very politicised. I often used to say that we had a parish magazine that was one page God business and three pages that were called 'on the industrial front'. We were right in the middle of it.

Geraldine: The great Labor split and so on?

Alannah: Yes, Arthur Calwell's sister was a nun at our high school. Bob Santamaria's niece was at the school. The DLP did very well at our parish.

Geraldine: Was ambition encouraged among girls?

Alannah: By my mother: absolutely. Oh God, my mother said she'd always felt that she hadn't made very wise choices in her life and she didn't want any of her daughters to make those same decisions. The very, very clear message was that you need to be independent, to rely on your own resources. You should never, ever put yourself in a position where you are dependent on a man. That was an unequivocal message. And the school leaders were women. So I was used to seeing women in positions of control. I remember one of my sisters was very keen to get married very early. My mother said, well, if you want the big white wedding, you're not going to have it until you've finished your nursing. You are going to get a qualification before I put one cent into a wedding.

Geraldine: So what role would you say work has played in your life? I'm really keen to work out how female leaders define balance in their life.

Alannah: I'm not sure that I would describe this as work. Without wanting to sound silly about it, I do think politics is not something you can say is work. I mean, it is a vocation so it's not like…

Geraldine: It's a calling?

Alannah: Yes, so there is no balance as far as that goes. You ask my children, who keep threatening to write the mummy-dearest book about how every night of their life I ring them up and say, sorry, I'm going to be late home…can you get the frozen lasagne out of the fridge? They supposedly can't remember any home-cooked meals. Never!

Geraldine: Do you whip yourself over that?

Alannah: Not particularly. I'm sure they're completely exaggerating. There are some other things that I whip myself over but, not that one. But being involved in politics in the Labor Party was intricately tied up with my life.

Geraldine: Your identity?

Alannah: I don't know about identity, but certainly life.

Her prevarication around the word 'identity' was interesting. It struck me during our meeting that Alannah wasn't especially introspective or reflective, not given to too much psychoanalysis. She has her legal background to enable her to grasp a brief quickly and assemble complex information tidily. She sees political activism as a calling, and she doesn't dwell on yesterday's mistakes or wounds. Maybe this three-fold suite of skills equips people particularly well for political leadership. Matt, her young advisor from Fremantle who escorts me through Parliament House to her office, says, 'She is incredibly tough, really, and she doesn't take politics personally.' Alannah believes in striding forward, not entirely without contemplation, but not racked by it either. In fact, the thing that could bring her undone is guilt at *not* having skin in the game.

Alannah: I would just feel too guilty all the time. I mean, I always feel guilty that I haven't done enough. I'm always analysing how I could have done more: I should have done this or should have done that. It's just the reality of some personalities. I don't think I could ever have not been involved; even at school, I was always involved in causes.

Geraldine: Are you conscious of a time when you decided to fulfil your potential related to this 'vocation', even if that meant some of your duties in other areas took a secondary role?

Alannah: Whether or not I quite understood it at the outset, there is always a compromise. It is true that you don't focus on your family in the same way that many other people do—well, I don't think one ignores them. But in a way, you are contributing to making a better society, which they are going to be part of. This is why sometimes I get a bit concerned about this question of 'family values'. If all you think about is your family and you don't take a view of the broader society, then it's not going to be a good place for anyone. I think one of the hallmarks of our civilisation and our tradition is that we do try to think beyond just our family. It's not all about family machismo. It's about how we move society as a whole forward and create a better, more open and fabulous environment for everyone to prosper in.

I wondered during our Parliament House chat whether she sincerely wished any personal trade-offs she'd made to be seen as noble and good. Was it possible to persuade yourself and others that the compromises between political and family life were a necessary by-product of trying to change the world? Would Bob Hawke's family consider they'd been blessed by their father's brilliant career? Would they have preferred a more mundane existence and had him around more?

Alannah: I don't think my situation has been anywhere near that complex. It does have its downside, and I certainly don't think either of my children would ever want to go into politics, absolutely not. I think you find two sorts: those who want to be part of the dynasty and those who don't, who wouldn't touch it with a ten-foot pole. I remember one night a very good friend of mine, Tom Stephens [ALP member for Kimberley, 2005–13] retired after thirty years in Parliament, and his wife got up and gave this absolutely best-ever spouse speech. She said, it has been an absolute privilege to be in this position. Now, she is an exceptional human being, but she said, the children and I have supported Tom in everything that he's done because we just think to have been out there representing the community is such an amazing privilege. I don't know whether my family would go that far, but I do think they appreciate the value of that work and that they take some pride in that.

But this question of trade-offs for a public life is very real. Alannah acknowledges that her husband, Perth lawyer Derek Schapper, paid the considerable price of loss of privacy in the small-city environment of Perth during the 2013 pre-election period. He was due to attend court over matters concerning his legal trust fund—which he'd self-reported and which normally would have not made headlines. Instead, Alannah publicly revealed details of the upcoming case during her press conference when she nominated for Perth, and, yes, the media was, naturally, straight onto him. The case was recently finalised. Schapper was fined and granted a spent conviction. Nevertheless, with the coverage in the *West Australian*, everyone knows about it now, regardless of the lack of record.

Alannah: Well I had a number of reasons I was a little reluctant to stand, and I discussed them with Derek, and he was very insistent that he understood that if I was going to stand I would have to reveal this. He said he was prepared for that to be the case.

Geraldine: That's impressive.

Alannah: It was very impressive. That's why I say that, although they're not necessarily attending events and things with me, my family has been very supportive.

Geraldine: So what about this word 'ruthless'? I'm asking because I have a view that women are terrified of that word being used to describe them, and yet it's arguable that you won't get to the top decision-making roles without a degree of ruthlessness. Do you see that in yourself? Does it worry you if you see it in yourself or if others describe you that way?

Alannah: Not really, because I don't think I am ruthless. I don't want to get into semantics, but if you look at ruthless, what does it mean? Without mercy. Now, sometimes you have to make tough decisions and sometimes you're presented with a number of options, and I would always like to think that I really do weigh up all the costs and benefits in making a decision towards what I consider a good quality outcome. I never feel I'm ruthless. I try to look at all of the difficulties and disadvantages that a certain decision might create.

Geraldine: You want to get your own way though?

Alannah: But I certainly don't want to do that at the expense of everyone else. If my husband had said to me, look I just don't think I could do that, I would have said, okay, I won't do it. I wouldn't have stood.

So here is a nice quinella: a conviction politician who nevertheless feels she could walk away if the requirements of the job compromised her soul. She has devoted much thought to why public life is important, but also to the skills required. I'm a real sucker for this. I yearn to see politicians actively cultivating the noble art of democratic politics: the capacity to dream, to think big, to trade, do deals, use good rhetoric, emphasise fairness, be wily and heal rather than divide. That's my personal list of key performance indicators—KPIs. I accept that the aim is to win, but not at all costs. Politics is like everyday life on speed, as one politician remarked to me during this research. Most of us wouldn't cop the pace well either. I admire much of the striving I see in many politicians. In fact the ritual baying for their blood, as if they're congenitally venal, depresses me. Alannah is convinced she has something to contribute in trying to be a voice for Western Australia, particularly on repositioning the climate-change discourse beyond its tedious left–right divisions, and on early childhood education. This area of Australian life appals her. She believes that the growing gap between lower-achieving children and the rest is entirely avoidable and needs a collective focus if Australia is to remain egalitarian in any sustainable way. I like the way she carefully analyses social and political issues, teasing them apart, so she can devise how to address them effectively with good policy, not just words.

Alannah: I am very interested in problem solving and policy implementation and I have developed, I think, the abilities to assess large amounts of information and to make judgments on how you would make progress on a matter—how to implement change. So I guess I've developed perhaps a bank of knowledge or an ability to understand the complexity of issues.

Geraldine: It doesn't frighten you?

Alannah: No. Having dealt with many, many complex issues,

I think what I can do is chart a way towards progress in solving problems, achieving better outcomes and making practical decisions: getting across the fundamental policy ideas and then also working on a practical implementation of a policy agenda.

Geraldine: Has your law degree helped you with that capacity?

Alannah: It has definitely, in terms of absorbing the brief, but also in making critical distinctions and being able to work through complex factual situations and work out which are actually critical issues. I did my first degree in philosophy, and that may have also been helpful.

Geraldine: So you've got a tidy mind?

Alannah: It's become tidier under the discipline. I think those intellectual disciplines do help you, regardless of how you might start off. I always want to see structures. I've always understood that about myself.

Geraldine: But do you get daunted when you're presented with a big problem that's multi-pronged?

Alannah: Well, I wouldn't like to explain something like string theory! But you don't start off with the most complex problem in politics—you acquire experience; you learn on the job. How can we set up this structure? What's the path? It's through the experience of actually working through practical problems which, to some extent, I was doing in law. Then in Opposition you have to get on top of very complex issues to come up with a plausible policy position. And in areas like, say, IT, I've still got an enormous amount to learn. I just think you have to constantly be keeping yourself up to date—with science and with other knowledge—and on the ball in how you get out and communicate that. You can't learn a particular suite of communication styles and techniques and expect that they're going to endure for life, not in a fluid community like ours. People are changing: the way they identify and take in information is changing very rapidly.

Geraldine: What about the role of rhetoric? That's where I see a real dearth of skills—people just not selling the message.

Alannah: It's about articulating the message. I don't know why people undervalue that as part of the job description of a politician and of a leader. To be able to succinctly describe an issue and a solution, and to inspire people about the path you want to embark on is incredibly important. That is what leadership is about. It's about bringing people along with you, whether or not you're a big man in a hunter-gatherer community or a prime minister of a country. How you go about forming your views and developing the relationship with the community involves another set of skills. But the ability to put the argument in a context that means something to people, and that they're engaged by, is incredibly important. Look at someone like Paul Keating. I mean he used to get people really interested in economics. He had an extraordinary and very visual way of describing complex economic issues and bringing them alive to people. So did Bob Menzies, he had great rhetorical skills.

So much of political persuasion is about projecting your confidence onto the people around you, Alannah believes, so that they step beyond partisan emotional divides, which are known and vaguely reassuring, into the riskier realm of change. It could be argued that this is more pressing for reform-minded parties like the ALP than more conservative groups, and harder to sustain within our current 24/7 news cycles. But this challenge gives Alannah oxygen, and she sallies forth in her inimitable way.

Alannah: I think part of the inspiring is being able to project that you actually deeply understand what it is you're talking about, because there'll be a certain percentage of people who don't want to spend the time to get fully across issues but want to be confident that the person they're investing their faith in has the ability to do the job.

Geraldine: Good point. I've become steadily more interested in this because I realise I haven't been very good at it myself. When I become persuaded of something that amounts to a change, I half expect others to just get it. I expect them to infer! I put the bones of it forward and can get quite frustrated when they don't grasp the pitch I'm making.

Alannah: Often it's really about changing the language and allowing people to become comfortable with an issue by seeing it from another, sometimes very different, perspective. For instance, in climate change, I think the big problem is that it's become a very partisan issue and if we just keep trying to sell it in the same way with more and more facts, we might not get across the line. So I guess in politics what you learn is that you have to try many different methods of getting your message across. And one of the advantages that you get in politics, too, is that you do hear people expressing a wide variety of views. So you're in a position to appreciate the complexity of human reaction to issues. Life becomes far less black and white when you're representing people who have very diverse political views.

Alannah's victory speech to ecstatic ALP workers and volunteers in Perth, on election night 2013, was simple and arresting. 'We will rebuild Labor!' The proof of the pudding will be in the eating, of course. Words are easy; follow-through is much harder, especially when trying to renovate complicated outfits like member-based political parties in twenty-first-century Australia. But listen to the way this political leader breaks down the challenges into bite-sized chunks both aspirational and *practical*, that word she emphasises so often.

Alannah: Well, I think that something like the rebuilding of Labor does require people to become enthusiastic and engaged. You're not going to rebuild if people are feeling disengaged, because it's really only with that sense of there being rank-and-file support that you're going to be able to get people who currently hold the power to loosen their grip on it. If you go in too modestly, you're just not going to create that energy, and without that energy, you're not going to get the change. You've got to aim high.

Geraldine: What about when you meet despair? You must have met that among your constituents?

Alannah: I always say this. If you've read a bit of history and looked at the beginning of the union movement and at the start of the movement for democracy, you'll have found there were people saying there was no hope for reform that time. There were people who would have argued

> then that the idea of universal male suffrage, let alone universal suffrage, was absolute pixieland, pie-in-the-sky, never going to happen. Seeing that those arguments are always put up to oppose change, and seeing that, with endurance and being prepared to make progress happen incrementally, change does occur. You know, that's history. The more you read history, the advances of civilisations, of science, the more you know there are always incremental steps, and occasionally there's a revolution. But change has always been made by people who have the persistence to hang in there.

Despite such clarity of purpose, Alannah knows well the caprice of tilting at political leadership: that advances are not guaranteed whatever the external signs, especially in Labor caucuses. Even when you think the numbers are on your side, things can change. In 2008, Labor premier Alan Carpenter stepped down after losing power to the Liberals' Colin Barnett, and the leadership became vacant. Wheeling and dealing was on, big time. Alannah had made considerable enemies in the West Australian union movement with her campaign to reduce the power of factional leaders and unions' rights to certain bloc-votes in caucus, a harbinger of more recent developments in the federal Labor party. However, she was widely regarded as the obvious candidate for opposition leader. But it didn't turn out that way. She decided not to stand at the last moment. The party opted for Eric Ripper, who'd been deputy premier and treasurer, and he went on to preside for three years before being ousted by the current leader, Mark McGowan. Alannah stepped back from active involvement in West Australian Labor in 2010, with some accusing her of leaving the parliamentary team at its moment of need.

Alannah: I made the strategic decision not to put my hand up [for the 2008 leadership ballot] if there was going to be a contest, because I understood how some of the forces would work. I knew that I needed to have a very broad base of support—otherwise, there would be certain people who would be systematically undermining me, and I wasn't prepared to take on the leadership under those circumstances. I was prepared to take it on, but I wanted there to be a consensus. I thought they made a wrong decision, and I thought the deal that was struck by Eric Ripper was bizarre because he'd rung me that morning and said, I've heard you've done a deal with the Left that you would agree to have Roger Cook, [the newly installed ALP member for Kwinana] as deputy. That's disgraceful, I said, of course I haven't done a deal like that, Eric. Of course I wouldn't do that, that's ridiculous to put Roger in, he's just come into Parliament. There'd be no reason why I would do that.

Then, lo and behold, someone rang and said, you've got the numbers; it looks like you're going to have that support. So then I get to Parliament at 9 am [to attend the leadership vote] and find that Eric had done the deal to have Cook as deputy. I just shook my head at him and he sent me a note, which I always wish I'd kept. It said it was okay for him but it wouldn't have been okay for me, which I thought was an interesting way of justifying something to yourself.

Geraldine: What does that do to you?

Alannah: I was absolutely astounded, but I wasn't hurt. I was gobsmacked by the audacity of it. I didn't have the feeling that I was passed over; but I wasn't prepared to accept any deal on the sort of basis on offer [of dropping her push for reform once in office].

Geraldine: But you couldn't win this group around; that's the interesting thing.

Alannah: I could have, if I'd said that I wasn't going to pursue any ideas of labour reform. What happened happened, and I can tell you I didn't feel passed over. I felt that the party had made a poor decision, and I think it contributed to losing the last election, because Eric had been there for three years and the community had already made up its mind that he wasn't going to be the leader. The ability of the party to really mount the attack on Barnett was limited. I thought electing Eric Ripper was the wrong decision, but I didn't feel personally aggrieved at that.

Geraldine: That's a real skill I reckon, not taking it personally.

Alannah: Well, there have been times in politics, when I was younger I guess, when I didn't get some sort of little position or something and it annoyed me. But no, I didn't take that personally. I suppose it was because I knew that I had the public's support. Also, I knew that I didn't fight hard for it. If I had fought hard for it…

Geraldine: Why didn't you?

Alannah: I suppose, I just know that if you come to leadership like that—it doesn't apply to everyone—but there were people in the party who would never ever support me and some of those would make it their mission to destroy me.

So, in a sense, this formidable woman did blink. She made a

decision about the terms of engagement, withdrew from the field and lived to fight another day. But, at the time, she lost, let there be no doubt about it. No matter what she now says, those white-knuckle power struggles leave deep scars on their combatants. I have yet to meet a woman who enjoys them, even vaguely, though I have certainly met a considerable number of men who seem to. Is it a well-founded fear of failure? Is it revulsion at the potential collateral damage caused by a fight to the (metaphorical) death? Is it a sudden realisation that nothing is quite worth that type of drama, short of defending your child or your physical life? It preoccupies me, I confess. And I don't enjoy the conclusion I'm drawing. Even women comfortable with their ambition, skills and ego may see dignified retreat as the best option. And they may well be right.

CHAPTER 5

SANDRA LEVY

A Passion to Produce

Sandra Levy AO intended to become a teacher after graduating from university with a bachelor of arts and a diploma of education. But after a traineeship in the ABC's education unit, her course was set for a lifetime career in television production at the public broadcaster, as well as at private production houses and, for a short time, Channel Nine. Sandra has been responsible for commissioning many television dramas and innovative documentary-style projects. She was the director of television at the ABC between 2001 and 2005, and is currently head of the Australian Film Television and Radio School.

ONCE, during the early 2000s, after I had compered an ABC Television launch party, Sandra Levy, who was head of TV, thanked me with possibly the biggest, most luxuriant bouquet of flowers that I've ever seen. That was typical Sandra. She'd micromanaged the gathering of scribes and critics to welcome the coming year. She had everyone jumping to attention—they were well aware of her legendary eye for detail. Woe betide anyone who dithered or was short of the same level of dedication. Her gimlet-eyed fastidiousness was ever present. Don't dare make a mistake, you yelled to yourself, not in front of Sandra! But when it was all over, she knew how to gush in true showbiz style, though with a touch of class.

Sandra Levy, now charged with training the next generation of producers in her role as head of the Australian Film Television and Radio School (AFTRS), is an incredibly interesting study. She is a woman with no doubts whatsoever about leading, as long as she's producing something worthwhile at the same time. The leadership process doesn't seem to fascinate her, but the product does. There must be a real yield for all the effort—otherwise, it's time to move on.

A battle-hardened veteran of the creative industries, Sandra says she cares little about her place in the hierarchy, but she is very much at ease making decisions. And big creative ideas need decision-makers to bring them to life. If others can make better decisions, she'll happily serve, or so she says.

Leading various Australian cultural institutions over the last thirty years has been her particular route to telling authentic Australian stories to the Australian people, her holy grail. Perpetually fascinated by ideas—creative visions, big dreams, either her own or others—she expects to argue passionately about them, to test their worth. She expects others will do the same and is shocked when they retreat. But she hates men shouting in anger at her when they could argue it out, if only they had the guts to try. Strangely, a lot of them don't even bother to talk to her seriously, she claims, even though she may sit in the adjacent office. Could they be frightened of her? Well they shouldn't be, she smartly counters. Then again, she prefers to be left alone to get on with it, preparing the production and design crews for the vital business of charting our culture.

Of course, most of us haven't had anything like the amazing foundation of Sandra's childhood, for which some of us may be grateful. She certainly was not bequeathed the notion of noble leadership—anything but. Her parents were communists from the Old World: a Russian-Jewish mother and an English-Jewish father, neither of whom 'were particularly involved parents' to her and her sister and brother. In fact, it was a 'weird family', she says, constantly out of step with the conservative community, yet hungering for acceptance, with her father an intellectual snob about education and learning, clothing and social trappings. The only real pride, in his eyes, was in being on the side of social change, certainly not in being one of the bosses. He was a colossal figure in her life and formation. Sandra knew that her role was to change the world; that was made explicit. So she grew up being interested in politics, knowing she had an obligation to demonstrate for causes and to 'make my position known'. A perfect training ground, I ventured, for future authority.

Sandra: No, for activism, not authority. If you think back on the 1950s and my parents' background—they never expected to become leaders. They were left-wing intellectuals in the Communist Party. They were not trade-union activists, so my growing up was dreamy and idealistic: reading Marx and reading about the Spanish Civil War and having left-wing book-club launches and supporting indigenous arts. So it was full of art and that sort of stuff.

My father was tough on us all intellectually. When we were little he was studying most of the time and we didn't see a lot of him. He would come to the table and he would say, who can spell and apply the word 'juxtaposition'? Who can apply and spell 'inchoate'? Did anyone notice there was a change of prime minister in Ceylon? This is when I was six and seven and eight. It was very confronting. But, I learned to argue and say things like, the massacre in Indonesia is unacceptable. And then we would argue about that. So, in a way, I think I had a pretty tough childhood.

He would always challenge us and make us defend our ideas, always. And now, as an adult, if I have a thought, I test it myself. I do a great deal of thinking. I over-prepare for everything, every meeting. I research everything. I want to know everything so that when I go in I am fully prepared. I wouldn't dream of going into a meeting without being fully prepared, and I expect other people to be too. I love the process, which I think is known as the dialectic of challenging ideas. I will argue a case just for the sake of arguing it, to make sure it hasn't got any holes in it. I love that process. I find it incredibly stimulating.

One of Sandra's duties as a senior public officer of the ABC required fronting a uniquely Australian inquisition, Senate Estimates committees, in Parliament House in Canberra. There, she and other colleagues were cross-examined by parliamentarians about their stewardship of the publicly funded entity. These experiences were usually intense: they have been known to reduce otherwise powerful men to apprehensive jellies. Sandra found them quite exciting. Not that she deluded herself she knew everything, despite her preparation. And by the sound of it, it wasn't merely the contest she relished, but the thrill of pitting herself against herself.

Her acute attention to detail, which is so useful in these sorts of meetings, probably helps inoculate her against the 'imposter syndrome' that can bedevil women. She simply never stumbles unprepared into anything. She is well armoured, with battle plans for most meetings.

Sandra: Maybe I'm more male than I know, but when I go into a meeting, I like to know what I would like the outcome to be. I hate the thought of going to a meeting and not knowing what it is that I am trying to achieve.

Geraldine: Like a chess strategy: they'll do that and I'll move there and then I'll do such and such?

Sandra: No, I couldn't do it that way. I don't think of it that way. I just think, okay, we're in a meeting where I want to, say, finance a film. Clearly what I want at the end of the meeting is for them to be positive about the project. What do I need to prepare in order for them to be positive? What sort of tastes have they got? What other projects might they have funded? How could I persuade them that this is going to be the sort of thing that would interest them? Or, if it's a meeting with a government representative and I need to convince them that the place is in good hands, I'll think about what sort of things they'll want to know: how we're managing it economically; what our strategies are. It's just doing the thinking, I suppose. I get nervous or tense before things, because I have everything thought out before I get there.

Were there any mentors for all this? She'd never had them, came the sharp reply, other than her father, who, with the wisdom of hindsight, she sees had left her a powerful legacy. By insisting she defend her case, he made Sandra formidably tough. He inadvertently set her up to cope with the blokeyness of television production and Senate Estimates and with on-the-make inquisitors from the world of politics. Not everyone thrives in this sort of environment, of course. During her directorship of the ABC TV division, Sandra's meetings became the subject of gossip, rather more persistent than the usual chitchat about aspects of management style. I didn't attend the meetings, but I remember the flavour of commentaries from people who did. Typically, there were those who admired her rigour, her sheer guts, like Andrew Denton, who told the *Age* newspaper in 2005 that he'd always found her 'direct and when need be, very tough', and that anyone who showed a sign of weakness in that job 'would have gone under quicker than the *Titanic*'.[5] He also noted her astuteness in only taking calculated risks, ensuring she was never too far out of her depth. But Andrew is one of the brightest sparks ever to cross the ABC doorstep. He'd have no trouble arguing his case. Whereas Sandra's critics said it took real guts to argue with her publicly around her big meeting table during pitching sessions. Dissenters would simply shut up, feeling it wasn't worth offering their concerns for discussion. So let's imagine, I said to Sandra, that I was a slightly timid but creative soul, attending one of your gatherings. Would I be invited to offer my response with an assurance that I would not be savaged should my thoughts not come out well?

> Sandra: Absolutely you would, I would say. But my own view is that some people are very uncomfortable articulating a position and uncomfortable defending a position; whereas I actually think it's just part of our role. If you're going to spend taxpayers' money, you want to make sure you have tested the idea fully and you've thrashed it out, if necessary, again and again and again.

Here's another surprise, born of her refreshing candour: Sandra is deeply suspicious of that most desired commodity, consensus. Most women aspiring to leadership believe the ability to broker consensus is one of the most powerful skills in their kitbag, offered without reservation as an asset. Not Sandra. Why ever not?

> Sandra: Consensus seems to me to be very confusing in the workplace. I think it is confused with easy agreement.

> You need to be able to articulate your thoughts and listen to arguments or to different ways to do something before making a decision. But, after all the arguments for and against, then you need to make a decision, even if not everyone agrees with it. When I say argument—I never lose my cool and I never swear and I'm never drunk—I'm interested in the exchange, and the people who do it with me enjoy it and we have lots of laughs. It can be terribly funny.

But warning signs flash for her if people demonstrate brittleness. If a producer making a pitch for a series set in the 1960s can't offer an original answer as to what interested him about that era, if his eyes glaze with panic at a touch of cross-examination, Sandra starts to worry. She likes people with emotional depth and strength, who've tested their ideas before advancing them. Then, she believes they're worth backing, and she will do so to the hilt. Perhaps dealing with Sandra requires gumption, a great Australian word derived from the Scottish, implying robust self-respect, a quality much encouraged by schools in the 1960s and 1970s. If you possess it, Sandra will be a remarkable enabler of your creativity. She will devote herself without reservation to bringing your ideas to life. But you had better be sure of yourself in the first place.

Sandra's intense focus makes me wonder whether it is something others could copy. It is partly derived from the parental expectations of her childhood, for which there have been observable costs. Without any prompting, she readily concedes a poignant reflection about her private life.

Sandra: I have basically had three botched relationships: two former marriages and one long de facto relationship.

> Clearly I am not good at that, I have to say. The evidence is in, I think. I am better at work than I am at my own life, so I just have to go with that.'

It probably didn't help that her partners were invariably working within the same, small professional pool. Maybe she got so accustomed to pulling levers at work and watching the wheels turn that she tried it at home. 'In fact,' she says, 'if you go into the house and issue instructions, basically all you do is annoy people, and they don't do it anyway!'

However, Sandra is proud of her mothering. She exercised her considerable discipline in the service of someone else and felt she did it very well. As a single mother, most of the time, she always got home early for her son, Simon, prioritising bath, dinnertime and bedtime stories. She would either go back to work at night or work late from home. Her payoff, other than the satisfaction of a maternal job well done, is a loving relationship with her adult son who is now thirty-four. Her other key, lasting relationship is with the writer Frank Moorhouse, a major 'intellectual companion in my life', forged in the libertarian 1970s, a time of sexual freedom and emotional independence.

But work has always been central in Sandra's life 'because it's not work, it's the things I love, which are writing and fiction and film and theatre. Work and my interests are the same thing really.' Lucky Sandra. It makes her a classic candidate for that psychological state called 'flow', identified by respected Chicago researcher Mihaly Csikszentmihalyi. Essentially, he found that when high-functioning people discovered such an effortless overlap between what could be characterised as 'work' and their inherent interests, they became so absorbed in the task that they were unaware of the passage of time. One activity supported the other without conscious effort in a way that advanced both enjoyment and effectiveness: they experienced 'flow'.[6]

Sandra's television career started with a traineeship in her twenties at the ABC, in its education section, building on her short-film-making experience at university. Then came one of those moments of serendipity, when she wandered into the drama department and simply knew she was home. Suddenly, it all made sense: all her interests in literature, film and art converged in this one creative magic box. Here was a place she belonged, where she found she was a natural decision-maker, full of confidence, comfortable with leading and producing, and not only in a management sense.

> Sandra: You have to have a lot of knowledge to produce drama. You have got to know a lot about production and ideas and writing and interpretation and genre. In other words, by the time I got to be a drama producer, in my early thirties or something, I had built up, maybe, fifteen years of seeing theatre and films and studying them and making them. So I had a fair amount of knowledge.
>
> Geraldine: So you're not a person of doubt?
>
> Sandra: No, not a lot, no. I might suffer regrets. I do make decisions very fast. Sometimes I look back and think it might have been better to dwell on that a bit more. But I get very excited about ideas. I get really passionate about something being the right thing to do. It's really exciting. I try to build the team and bring them with me, so that doesn't leave a lot of room for doubt, not if you are going to be a visionary leader of some kind, which I would never have seen myself as, but, looking back, it might be true.

Even so, conditions need to be right to foster leadership, however talented a person may be: that's one of the key lessons to take from Sandra's story. Just because you succeed in one arena, there are no guarantees about moving to another, absolutely none.

In 2005 Sandra left the ABC, with huge successes under her belt, such as the comedy series *Kath and Kim* and the interview series *Enough Rope*. She had also poached Margaret Pomeranz and David Stratton from SBS and boosted the ABC's prime-time audience share by twenty-one per cent. Nevertheless, her reign was also marked by big internal stoushes with the powerful news department, some of whose executives felt Sandra was not collegial enough or sufficiently amenable to allowing breaking stories to disrupt the nightly television schedule. Sandra emphatically denies the accusation, but it proved terrific fodder for the headline-writers, especially in the Murdoch press: nothing much has changed there. As television writer Catherine Keenan put it, Sandra was often painted as 'a sort of Attila the Hun in designer clothes...the sort who might eat her young'.

Over time, these scrappy tussles stung too much. Sandra felt she'd been hung out to dry as the scapegoat in yet another episode of fevered turmoil at the national broadcaster. So, after being personally approached by Kerry Packer, she moved to Channel Nine as head of programming and development with the brief to introduce some new ideas into the network in the post Alan Bond era. It seemed a great opportunity. But she now describes it as 'five of the worst months of my life'. For all her experience and toughness, the tribal nature of commercial television and its different priorities tripped her up. It left some scars, which took time to heal. Moving between networks, as I can attest to, is a highly challenging venture. All four—ABC, Seven, Nine and Ten—are in the same basic business: transmitting images and sound to the Australian population, to both inform and entertain. But they've each carved out distinct segments of the community; they tailor their product accordingly and describe their core missions quite idiosyncratically. Sandra realised she did not belong at Nine, hating every second of it, and got out of there as fast as she could.

Sandra: Well they didn't want me there for a start. It was only Kerry Packer and Sam Chisolm [Packer's legendary CEO] who wanted me there, but the rest of management didn't. I was caught in an impossible situation, which I sort of knew on day one: I had no budget, no staff, no schedule. The job that I thought Kerry wanted me to do was basically to fix the network. But when I got there I found that Sam hadn't even told people I was coming. He hadn't defined the job. There was no office for me. So I walked in and Michael Healy, who was programmer at that time, said, oh, this is trouble. It was a complete disaster.

Geraldine: But this experience didn't undermine your sense of yourself by the sound of it, or did it?

Sandra: It knocked me a bit. I thought, okay, what I need to do now is win their trust. There were a few people who I thought would gradually let me do more things if I won their trust. I didn't doubt that I knew how to fix their network. I thought it was very old fashioned and testosterone-ridden. They hadn't understood women or young audiences, and I had things I would have done if they'd let me. By the time I left, I felt a bit wounded. And also, when I left the ABC, which I should never have done, my father had just died, and Michael, my husband whom I was separated from but still very close to, had just died slowly [of pancreatic cancer]. And I only took a couple of days off. So I had two recent and sad deaths to deal with and I was being knocked around by the *Australian*, which I had been for years. [The national newspaper relentlessly covered both large and small details of her ABC decision-making, highlighting her detractors and their criticism and rarely outlining her successes. The criticism was often strident and personal, with descriptions of her as the public broadcaster's dragon-lady.] I thought ABC management could have publicly defended me more by answering them.

I was completely exhausted when Kerry started saying come and work for me. I probably should have said, no, I need a holiday. I didn't have the good sense at that time to say to myself, just take a break, just go away for a few weeks and recover. Sometimes you look back on your life and think, oh, I know what I should have done then. But I thought, if I work harder and take on more and more projects, it will be fine. But no. Nine was an awful aberration. I felt like I had been completely stupid and made an appalling decision to go there. I couldn't believe I had been so silly. And then, because I walked out, sort of begging to get out of the contract, I had no money and I didn't have anything lined up. I hadn't planned to be unemployed and without any projects. So it was a bit of a shock.

A searing shock, in fact. And we hadn't discussed the issue of aggressive alpha males, a well-known feature of the Nine

Network, admittedly part of its legendary strength when it reigned supreme in Australian television from the early 1990s till the mid 2000s. Sandra won't go into details, but she viscerally shudders remembering the language and shouting she routinely encountered. It knocked her off her moorings—she who'd long been accustomed to being the only female producer on teams at the ABC and other production houses she worked with. But the tone at Nine was different, especially the male anger, some of which she thought simply masked incompetence and uncertainty about where to go next.

Sandra: I like working with men, but I prefer working with a mix of both genders. I don't want to work with single-gender groups; I don't think it is good, but, no, I'm not intimidated by men. But it wasn't just alpha males—I've been on boards with David Gonski, the prominent business figure who now chairs the ANZ bank among many key positions, and the late James Strong, formerly chair of Qantas, both charming people. David is very powerful, very effective, but couldn't be sweeter in the way he runs a meeting. As was James. Joe Skrzynski, formerly chair of the Sydney Opera House, was my executive producer on *High Tide* [with Judy Davis], and, again, Joe is a charming man.

Men who are powerful don't all come in the same packaging. And the thing about the ones who are rude and unpleasant is that, in a way, one immediately loses respect for them. The ones I've worked for who I found really delightful, immensely successful and capable and high achieving, don't strut their stuff.

Management, in Sandra's view, needs to be both sophisticated and principled. She says she has always prioritised getting things done over what she terms 'motherhood statements'—words that don't outline how you and your group will actually get there. Even her detractors concede that you can rely on Sandra to be pragmatic and to prioritise activating productions rather than waiting around, sometimes for months and years, for the perfect conditions to arrive. Once production starts, morale lifts because the complex teamwork that is required to produce television simply dominates people's lives. Idle hands and equipment are not acceptable, in Sandra's eyes. After years of watching the tendency to delay in commissioning teams in television, I really admire Sandra's drive to get going. I believe that properly articulated visions by people in authority really do matter to those working for them. These statements, in effect, offer people a reason to turn up to work, beyond merely collecting a wage, because someone in authority knows where they are going. It is very inviting.

Another principle Sandra has always applied is to figure out what's missing in the workplace and then devise a way to deliver it. Years ago, when she arrived back at the ABC after working outside, there was little internal production underway and little fresh content. Endless English comedy repeats at 6.30 pm, just before the main news bulletin, didn't strike her as a valid representation of modern Australia—there was something missing. So she set about the formidable task of recruiting crews and production units across the country for the *New Dimensions* series, which ran for two seasons. The episodes were spread across the week and offered a magazine-style coverage of everything from health to finance to volunteerism. These days, what's missing at AFTRS, she notes, is students' understanding of the intellectual and creative history of the ideas that drive the industry they're trying to enter.

Sandra: So I'm building that into the courses. We're adding a major course called History of Film, which is really the scholarship of film. I don't understand how young filmmakers can't have proper references back to the history of film, a different genre, different periods and modes of storytelling. I know most of them don't go to theatre and they don't read books. And I think, how do they get by? Where is the stimulus coming from? What is going into the head? And I look at some of their material—some of it is so derivative and shallow. You might say, well with new technology they can make anything any time, they're constantly busy, they've got access to laptops with editing programs, music programs. But what's missing is the cerebral bit. So let's build that up. I have a public program of screenings and interviews every Friday and a regular journal of ideas and all sorts of other things. I try to work out what bits are working well and why and the context and then what is missing. And I bring people in to join me in it. Sometimes I'm not as good on consensus as I probably should be, but I am getting better at it.

Geraldine: What about the sociability required of the modern leader?

Sandra: I'm a disaster at that stuff. If we want to talk about things I'm bad at, I really hate small talk and socialising. I'm not good at it. I'm insecure about it. I get in a flap about it. To have to go and make small talk for a night fills me with anxiety.

Geraldine: Like the Christmas party here at the school?

Sandra: That stuff makes me sick to the stomach, whereas the stuff about coming up with a new strategy and what we should be doing and how to raise money—none of that bothers me. But the socialising at a party: I've been known to get to the door and then turn back and think, no, I can't face it.

Geraldine: And what about the big speech and the rhetoric, drawing people in?

Sandra: No, I'm not a natural at that either. I just like to quietly get on with it. I don't like the visible parts of leadership. It has to be done, but I don't like it. I'm tremendously shy in my own private life. If you asked me the same questions about my own life, my answers would be quite different from those about my work life.

Sandra always specifically employs ambitious young women as her assistants, assuming they'd like to become producers. She has mentored many of them, and she actively encourages female students to aim high. One of them told her recently how wonderful it was having her at AFTRS as a role model, as a strong, independent female leader. Sandra thought it was sad that, after all this time, young women still needed to think like that.

Then again, watching Julia Gillard as prime minister was sobering for this veteran activist. Despite believing that the former prime minister did not always show good judgment or communicate her message ideally, the Levy verdict is that the woman was judged by different standards. For a start, Sandra insists, she would never have run the ABC TV series *At Home with Julia*, a parody of the domestic life of the prime minister and her partner, Tim Mathieson.

Sandra: I thought it was disgusting. I was very angry with the ABC. I thought, you are poking fun at her as an object. This is not political humour. This is no *Yes, Minister.* I had never liked to think that we were a misogynist society because I thought, well, I've had a good career; there's nothing I haven't been able to do. But over the years, the longer I'm around, the more I think we are a society that is very, very uncomfortable with women and very mistrustful of women, very willing to judge them harshly and to treat them as second-class people. I don't think the Gillard era set things back, because I don't think we've advanced too far anyway! I just don't think there is any sense in Australia that women are complex, interesting people in the same way men are.

One of the benefits of a big, well-lived, warts-and-all life is how it frees people from regret, from the sense of having missed out on something somewhere along the line. Well, Sandra has personally tested this theory, with a health scare that I suspect turned out to be liberating—surprisingly so—for her. Two years ago she was diagnosed with a brain tumour. Doctors said they'd have to operate: they didn't know how big the tumour was, whether she'd emerge with brain damage, or even whether she'd emerge alive.

Sandra: I dream a lot, and I think I sort things out through dreaming and thinking at night. Before I had the operation, I had to grapple a lot with questions like, what if I died? Or what if I wasn't me anymore? And I remember on the way to the hospital in the morning there was a very, very heavy fog. My son had stayed overnight with me and drove me to the hospital. I felt very calm, and thought, well, if I'm dying and I'm going to die I don't really have any regrets. I've lived the life I chose. I feel okay. It was a quite calm feeling, a nice feeling.

Geraldine: So you felt you did emerge as you?

Sandra: On the day of the operation, of course, I was terrified, and when I came out of the anaesthetic in the intensive-care ward, I heard myself arguing with the nurse about what the blood-pressure readings were, and I thought, oh thank God, it's me!

She's back, they all yelled with relief. Back to lead uncompromisingly, to demand a lot from those around her, and to do it her way.

CHAPTER 6

SUE MORPHET

Risk and Reinvention

Sue Morphet intended to devote herself to teaching, having left university with a bachelor of science and a diploma of education. But her father's death propelled her into the family business, and she has remained in the world of commerce. Her career bloomed during almost twenty years at the Melbourne-based manufacturer Pacific Brands in a range of roles, culminating in CEO. She has now moved beyond management duties to the membership of various boards, private and public, and is chair of the peak body Manufacturing Australia.

IT should be a truth universally acknowledged that a modern, talented woman in search of a challenge can stumble headlong into the marketplace at its most capricious and vicious. For Melbourne businesswoman Sue Morphet, stepping up to leadership late in 2008, at just about the worst time imaginable, was transformative. Hers is a story of being at the helm when the going is unbearably tough. And no amount of rehearsal can prepare the woman, or those who love her, for the experience of being stretched to breaking point; of finding oneself in a predicament entirely outside the normal range, a bit like confronting a massive firestorm rather than merely bushfires. Yet there she was, before everything erupted, relishing the challenge of the top job at the veteran manufacturer Pacific Brands, producer of Australian staples such as Sheridan sheets, KingGee shorts, Bonds undies, Berlei bras and Hush Puppie shoes. She'd served a long apprenticeship in middle management. She knew an awful lot about the company, or so she thought.

But this was the year that ushered in the GFC, the most serious crisis in the international economy for many years. Did she seriously consider the gathering winds when moving from head of Underwear and Hosiery, just one branch of this conglomerate company, to CEO? Did she simply believe she would prevail? Did she have any inkling of the financial tsunami that would engulf the company and the epic 'whoosh' that would sweep up her and her family, making her a household name in February 2009? Sue followed the strict ASX rules of disclosure and formally announced she was laying off twenty per cent of the employees and shifting production of some of our best-known brands to China. At the same time, it was announced that in her move to CEO, her salary would triple, to $1.8 million. Her predecessor had reportedly earned about double that, and she had been promoted to a much higher level of responsibility from that of her previous job. But those details were lost. The staggering gulf between the executives, exemplified by Sue, and the retrenched workers from working-class Melbourne and Sydney suburbs (1800 of them) made headlines.

So much for Australian egalitarianism, raged the talk round the country—including, I confess, in my own home. So much for women representing some loftier set of goals about a fair distribution of wealth; they'll grab for themselves, like any good atavist, even during a team crisis, was the feeling. Unforgivable. Un-Australian. Certainly, as the current *Australian* newspaper editor Clive Mathieson wrote at the time in the *Punch*: 'Too little was made of the 7000 jobs the drastic measures were designed to save. And, at times, in the days that followed, Pacific Brands appeared flat-footed, almost surprised, by the venom of the media campaign against the job cuts and, particularly, Morphet's pay.'

Sue Morphet is one of the most deeply committed business citizens I've met. She adores the world of commerce, accepts its rigours and its caprice, and is happy to devote her energies to it. She is no Macquarie-Bank-style big dealmaker; neither is she a bleeding heart. She believes in being a good employer, but swears by her small-businessman father's dictum: if you look after the business, the business will look after the people it can afford to employ. This credo helped her, as she sees it, to divorce herself from the sky-high emotions that characterised the 2009 crisis.

> Sue: We were able to build plans and retraining programs and all that sort of stuff, so you don't ignore the people, but number one, you have to make the decisions that are right for the business, and then the business can do its job. You need to treat it like a living, breathing thing.

Sue is the eldest of six children who grew up supported by a bakery business. It's as if she was brought up to believe that business, as the saying goes, was a stand-alone exercise, free of politics and emotions. Yet she was no ingenue. Business was discussed around the Morphet family dinner table constantly. She learned her love of product by watching her father examine each bread loaf about to be consumed. And she experienced first-hand his management of personnel, always complex in a 24/7 operation. Lots of good lessons were learned.

Somehow though, none of it mattered when she found herself confronting a set of company books at Pacific Brands that were built for a bull rather than a bear market. She'd managed just one division, Underwear and Hosiery, where she'd built the 'capabilities…and I assumed we had similar capabilities across the rest of our business, but we didn't'. So, very early in her term as CEO, Sue grasped that she'd need to shut factories and lay off staff. That was hardly easy, but it was quickly overshadowed by the demands of the subsequent controversy it led to.

Mayhem reigned. The media smelled blood. This propelled another set of problems into the foreground. What to do now? Try to circuit-break the heightened emotions that contained more than a touch of schadenfreude and were spilling out everywhere? Or lie low and let the worst of the crisis blow itself out? Anyone tilting at leadership in any form in Australia is faced with this dilemma at some point, so it's important to formulate a strategy that might work. A few super-canny types manage to ride it out and even thrive. I recall hearing some wise words, a few years ago, about managing a crisis from a smart public bureaucrat, Dr Don Weatherburn of the New South Wales Bureau of Crime Statistics. If you could withstand the heat of a genuine controversy, he told conference delegates, you could achieve disproportionately big changes in public policy. However, usually controversy was too tough to manage and should be avoided. Sue was advised to 'just keep my head down and get on with it', which she generally abided by, until she decided to do a Nine Network *60 Minutes* interview in March 2009, in a segment titled 'The Boss', which some believe changed everything.

Sue: I had to do something. I think the counsel given in the first instance was just don't respond. Just keep going, don't respond. Otherwise, you enter into a conversation and the whole thing blows up. But then not responding had its impact. The reason that I did the *60 Minutes* interview was that my staff needed to see me out there; they needed to see that I was going to stand up to the criticism on their behalf, because it was extremely difficult for the company, as much as it was difficult for me. As a matter of fact it was worse for them. It's a bit like when you're having a baby: you're getting on with the job, whereas for the people who are standing around it's appalling. And this instance was the same: the staff and their families were going through an horrendous period. We had people going to the supermarket—many with logos on their shirts because they worked in the warehouse—and people would say at the checkout, how many jobs have you got rid of this week, mate? Stuff like that. So, I did *60 Minutes* for that reason. When I finished the interview I thought I was going to vomit.

I was beside myself. You get pushed and pushed and pushed in an interview to a point where you know it raises your emotions, almost to an anger level. And I thought, this eight weeks has been hard enough. I actually lost some trust in the media.

As she outlined the experience to me in Melbourne, nearly five years later, I shuddered. The pressure she must have experienced is indescribable. Some was probably self-inflicted. Some of it was outright unfair. But it was all real, and it had to be survived.

Sue: It's all well and good for people to say, did we think about the appearances? We didn't have any time to think about the appearances. We went from a company that bought businesses to deliver growth to one that had an $800-million debt in a very difficult market with the dollar going down, making our products more expensive to produce. We hit a perfect storm in a matter of months, not a matter of years. In October 2008, we were first to flag that there was going to be a downturn, because we were so close to the market. We sold socks and underpants. People stop buying socks and underpants when something is going wrong. And if they are not buying overalls, then it means their tradie business isn't going so well. We were right at the coalface. So, in October we could tell that things weren't as strong as we would have liked. By the time we got to November, the banks were starting to tighten, and we had to refinance $800 million.

Geraldine: Nightmare!

Sue: We were a wholesale company selling stuff that could be equally transferred to house brands. From November to January—six weeks—we had to devise a plan for the banks that would deliver $200 million worth of savings in a company that was probably going to be very badly hit by the GFC. We worked over Christmas. We had already developed a strategy to build the company's strength, but I jolly well thought that we were going to do that over three years, for goodness sake, not over six weeks! The banks were in an extremely tight market themselves, and when our results came out in February, I had to go to market and tell the analysts that we needed to remove significant costs and that we only had the backing of our banks for six months. Well, they could just see straight through that, that someone wasn't backing us, and our share price dropped to twelve cents [from the pre-GFC peak of $3.50]. We didn't have time to worry about whether Sue Morphet was earning $700,000 or $3 million. We had to worry about whether or not we were going to get these banks over the line. And, while all this storm was going, underneath it…

Geraldine: You were involved in a business SES operation?

Sue: We were, and my family knew that, I knew that, and the vast majority of our staff knew that. And that's why we weathered the storm, we just kept going, and the day we got the fourth bank over the line was an extraordinary day. Our share price then went to 35 cents and then we got on with it and took the $200 million worth of costs out of the business. So there you go. It was fascinating.

But as Sue reduced the number of brands from 300 to forty, and the distribution centres from thirty-seven to thirteen, the collateral impact on her personal life was considerable.

Geraldine: You had to put in security guards, at home too?

Sue: We had helicopters going over our house—we had our house on television and in the media. There were posters on the telephone poles in Hawthorn saying 'remove the corporate thief from our neighbourhood' with my photo on them. It was appalling. My husband and I and our son, who lived at home at the time, moved in with my daughter for ten days. We changed our phone number, the whole thing. It was appalling, and it was hard for my family. It was very hard for my family, full stop.

Geraldine: Was there a point when you consciously thought to yourself: I'm carrying on, no matter what the cost?

Sue: Absolutely. There was no time when I thought this would beat me.

Geraldine: Even if your family is being crunched?

Sue: There is no doubt it was tough on my family. But I don't think it would have been any less tough if I'd given in.

Geraldine: Did you ask them about that?

Sue: No, but I don't think they would have wanted that either. They just wanted it to be over. My kids were really happy after something like six months: one of them said, I've been to a party and no one asked me about Pacific Brands or you. And my husband said, I've been down to the local store and no one said, I saw your wife in the paper again, or offered their opinion on what you should be doing. There was none of that, after a period of time.

Geraldine: Did you have a little council of war with them?

Sue: Oh, yes, of course we did. We didn't all agree all the time on what should be done. We had plenty of heated discussions in the household about what should have been done. It was hard because they were adults and everyone had an opinion and because they were being emotionally turned upside down by it. So yes, it was intense.

Ironically, Sue had obeyed all the 'rules' offered so readily by business columnists: control costs, remove emotion and sentimentality from your decision-making, assess the core mission. She embodied all those lines about the good leadership required to take Australia into the Asian century. She listened, applied the harsh medicine and, frankly, got little thanks. The business, five years on, is alive, but it's not exactly flourishing.

Sue has a good new position as chair of the peak body Manufacturing Australia, an organisation about which she is passionate and which represents a sector wrestling with its position in the economy. She also has significant board appointments that are taking her into new territory. Her role these days is charged more with influencing the public agenda than producing the tangible products she so loves. She has a great start-up idea, but wouldn't share details just yet, intending to have everything in place before she reveals all. She has learned some big lessons about public disclosure in the hardest of ways. However, she's very excited about the portfolio she's building. 'I believe I've got one more creative chapter left in business,' she declares. Board work, to her surprise, is anything but dull. She is enjoying the complexity of throwing herself into different businesses. I hope this reborn businesswoman will attract fellow investors to collaborate in that next stage.

There is one undeniable benefit of her new life, so far removed from the turbulent times, and that's personal flexibility. I wonder whether this, rather than leadership itself, is the glittering prize of a well-lived life. But is personal flexibility really possible alongside a modern leadership role, with all the glare of public scrutiny and market expectations? Or is it the trade-off that dare not speak its name? We're told frequently that most of us harbour 'leaders within', just waiting to be discovered. But how many of us wish to be so hemmed in regarding our time and choices, and our precious liberty?

Not one of the women I interviewed regretted her choices. Research pioneered by Sir Michael Marmot concluded that the more you perceive yourself in charge of your fate, the healthier you're likely to be. This classic work, on British civil servants, shifted the debate profoundly; it found that higher positions in the power hierarchy corresponded with better individual health. Instead of seniority producing rampant stress and terrible consequences (as the orthodoxy had suggested), lower-ranked workers, who felt much less in control of their lives, were more sickly than their superiors.[7] Overall, possessing power and influence is good for your health!

> Sue: I've very rapidly got used to flexibility after being a CEO and having none of it. I like the flexibility of thought and of time that I haven't had since I was at university, because I've always been in one field or another where your time and your thinking is dominated by one theme.
>
> Geraldine: Well, you've had to be very disciplined.
>
> Sue: Oh, definitely. I am enjoying my life now, particularly that I can actually put the pen down at three o'clock on a Friday and go and start enjoying my weekend, without the mad rush that accompanies the lives of working mothers come Saturday morning—getting your hair done, turning your house back into a home, you know that feeling? I'm enjoying that a lot but I'm also liking the fact that I can start to give back to the community. I've got that room in my life.

All in all, Sue believes she's had a very good year, after stepping down from outright leadership, despite the recent sadness of losing her mother. The year was marked by something she'd previously had neither the time nor maybe the inclination for, hadn't even registered that it was useful: she joined an Australian trade delegation to Europe for a week, led by then governor-general Quentin Bryce and including other members of the European Australian Business Council. Her delight in experiencing this totally different side of business was rewarding to see.

> Sue: It was absolutely fascinating. I loved it. I learned about Europe from the inside out. We met the president of the European Union in its conference room with all

the translation booths. We went to Slovakia with the governor-general, which was like going with the Queen to Bendigo. It was marvellous.

Geraldine: And I presume you had a secretariat, and all that formal help that the government provides.

Sue: Absolutely. It was a terrific learning experience. From Manufacturing Australia I've learnt how policy development either works or doesn't work in Canberra, how you go about it, how you lobby, who's powerful, and how advocacy works in the seat of power, none of which I knew before. It's been almost like a gap year for me. I've learnt a lot about how government works and I love being part of the public debate. I love all that. I've begun to love reading the papers again of a morning: who's saying what to whom and what are they doing and why are they doing it, and what are they doing about it? Isn't the message clear enough or loud enough or to the right person or is no one listening? So when you are head down—I'm going to say as a working mother—a lot of this stuff just stays too far away from your thought process.

Geraldine: Because you just haven't got the room for it?

Sue: You don't make the room for it because you are making the room for understanding only what you need to. You're consumed with understanding your family and the job and managing staff and so on. Unless your business is associated with political issues, you're pretty well focused on the job at hand, more so than on the industry at large.

Some of the commentaries on Sue's departure suggested that she might find it harder to reinvent herself than some senior men had, that women didn't achieve this as easily as men. These big exits can turn out to be significant personal tipping points. Kelly Magowan, an executive career coach, has seen several talented executives re-evaluate their whole careers at this stage, questioning what it was all about, quite seriously, for the first time in their lives. Might Sue fit this mould?

Sue: I'm not sure about whether men are better are reinventing themselves than women. But I have to say that I am not reinventing myself—you are who you are—but I am actually progressing to the next step of my career. When you're in your late fifties you're probably going to build on where you are, rather than reinvent who you are. I'm really hoping that the next twenty years builds on the last twenty.

Geraldine: I wonder if there is more at stake for women than for men in leaving a company like Pacific Brands, where you've made relationships and invested such a lot in them?

Sue: There may well be. I think the one thing for women who get to an age like me, their late fifties, and have raised children as well as a business, is that there is very little stop time on that journey. You are actually doing two jobs the whole way through, and I didn't realise just how tired I was. Even though I had the energy for work, as the pressure builds you run on adrenaline. Nothing stops. It's 24/7, and certainly the first eighteen months of my tenureship as CEO were extraordinarily intense, and you don't have time to actually recover from that. You just have time to deal with it and then push it aside and keep going, and it's tough. I'm not feeling sorry for myself. That's just the way it was. You regroup and get on.

I was fortunate that I was able to build a very good team of people, and, as a good team builds, it takes a lot of the pressure. But at the end of it, nevertheless, it is like taking off shoes that you've got used to hurting your feet. You take them off and your feet start to throb and you think, I could have probably stood up in those shoes for a while yet, or I could have walked another few kilometres. But I didn't realise how tired I was until I took my shoes off. I remember the naturopath saying to me, you will be tired for six months, Sue. Don't ask of your body any more than that. You will be tired for six months. And I was.

Geraldine: What makes a strong leader? The research suggests you have to prime yourself for leadership, because it rarely arrives unheralded. And that a psychological repositioning is critical.

Sue: I don't believe you wake up thinking, I'm a great leader, and now I'm going to go out and lead. You become good at leadership because of who you are and what you do. Experience teaches you the rest. That said, I do think you can enhance your leadership skills, most definitely. There are plenty of things that I could have done differently. With hindsight, I think about the mistakes I made, that I should have picked up on and probably would never do again.

Geraldine: Could you name one?

Sue: Well, I would like to think that I stood up for my team whenever it was appropriate to do so. But I sometimes question whether I always did as well as I should have. Big business can sometimes be intimidating. When I reflect,

I think my big learning from that time was not to be intimidated.

Geraldine: Each of the women, bar one, I interviewed has said something like that. It's most interesting, that they have retreated from the ultimate fight.

Sue: If I close my eyes and think, what was my biggest failing, it was that aspect. And yet I pushed so hard, and I fought tough fights, very tough fights that many others wouldn't have fought. But there were some that I just couldn't get through, and I think that never again would I do that. I've learnt. I feel much more capable. I just wouldn't let it happen again.

Geraldine: But did you retreat?

Sue: Not so much retreat. But there were a couple of things that, instead of taking six weeks to get through, took me two years. Mind you, at the same time, boards have got to be able to push back. I'm very aware of that. Many times it's about going back and reworking, reframing, and that can be both time-consuming and morale-dampening. What's more, people look to a CEO to be able to push down all barriers. So that's my biggest heartache and reflection. Funny isn't it? I mean there were just two or three things that I was unable to get through. One I finally got through, but it took me eighteen months of going back, reworking, redoing, all that sort of stuff. And I wonder if things would have been different if I'd have got it through in a year instead of eighteen months.

Geraldine: Well you could have threatened to resign, of course. It's that high-stakes play isn't it?

Sue: I wondered about that too. You think, well, I've got a family, and this is the job that I do, so fix the damn problem! I think that's one of the things that I do—my daughters say the same thing. The one thing we always do in our household is we always solve the damn problems. We don't walk away. I think that's the characteristic that I probably exhibited, instead of saying, it's either me or that.

Could there be an important distinction right there that needs naming? Sue is not a classic entrepreneur with a my-way-or-the-highway conviction about the next big development, or she hasn't been up till now. She is more an organic builder of traditional businesses, with a quite complex and developed view of the reciprocity involved in, what I'd consider to be, good capitalism.

Sue: When you are in business, particularly with big trading partners, you've got to leave a dollar on the table for every man: everyone's got to make a dollar out of the trade; otherwise, business fails. It mightn't fail on that deal, but it will on the next one or the one after that. You do need to take into account the expertise that would be sitting around in a boardroom as well as the expertise that's sitting around in management. It's a type of double act.

This sums up Sue's approach to her craft. So questions like bringing women on—'I had a team of very good women; my predecessor, Paul Moore, set up an environment that was good for women'—or dealing with alpha males related to merely second-rank issues that required clear decisions, but barely raised her temperature.

Sue: Alpha males? Oh, I've dealt with them on my life's journey, you have to. They are there. They're a challenge, but as someone very dear to me said, Sue, learn to manage thoroughbreds—they're fabulous if you can harness them. I think that you've actually got to like working together. You don't want to have bullies in your team. The good thing about being a CEO is that you can weed them out, and you do. It's not easy, because sometimes they come with a lot of skills. And you do have some people who are hard work: that's a thoroughbred thing. And there are some female bullies too. They're not worth having on your team for any reason, because you'll never get the employees underneath them to blossom. You're better off with someone who might not be as talented but who can manage the team.

As for the atmospherics, the 'right look' for a Melbourne gal who wants to lead: well, Sue has that down pat, with her cool, black garments. Television viewers came to expect a stylish, calm presentation. She sought to be as well presented, as she puts it, as would be expected of a man. She believed it was not right to look tired, even if she was. Her team did not expect her to be a show pony, but they did expect a certain standard to be maintained. And this had its funny side.

Sue: It's why we all wear suits! You have a uniform. It has to be reasonably accessible and varied. You just put on this suit today, that suit tomorrow, and the next, the next—like men have shirts and ties, women in business, unfortunately, have to have a number of suits. As the CEO, there's not one moment in the day that you can't be ready to do something that requires you to have a jacket on, every day. You have to go to work knowing that if you needed to see the bank or make a presentation or do something at short notice, you are well equipped. Every day.

Geraldine: Did you sometimes just wake up thinking aaagh, with the putting on the makeup and so on?

Sue: The whole box and dice. That was part of the job. My son said to me, I just thought it was normal that every household had to go through the drama of the hair, the suit, the lipstick, high heels and briefcase as well as everything else in the morning. And I know this is girls' talk, but you find the manicurist who can come to your home after dinner and she gets to know the kids, and you have someone come and cut and blow-dry your hair at home, because not only do you need to do most of those things after hours, but if you do it at home, then even if you are working out of your briefcase, you are still at home.

Geraldine: On their territory.

Sue: Yes, and they don't care what you do when you're at home, as long as you're at home. Except talk on the mobile phone—they hate that. I would always try very hard to use the mobile phone in the car before I went inside.

How well I remember that: my children's sudden descent into naughtiness when I found myself on the mobile at home. I developed a phobia that lasted for years about these calls.

Sue doesn't appear too scarred by her brush with fame as a leader in corporate Australia. But she is not rushing back there either. It was searing for a while. However, she does recognise herself, and her family recognises her too. This is her proud achievement.

CHAPTER 7

GAI WATERHOUSE

'I Did It My Way'

Gai Waterhouse, one of Australia's most successful racehorse trainers, has been in the business as a trainer since 1992. Her racing business, based at Tulloch Lodge, has steadily expanded and now employs more than ninety people. In 2002–03 Gai equalled her famous father T. J. Smith's Sydney record of 156 wins in a season, and in 2013 she won the Melbourne Cup with Fiorente. In 2000 Gai was the New South Wales Businesswoman of the Year, and she has been listed as a National Trust Living National Treasure.

WAS Gai Waterhouse pulling my leg, as racing people often do? Was that little trophy adorning our luncheon table the real deal, the 2013 Melbourne Cup awarded to the winning trainer just weeks before? Ohmigod, it was! I almost fell off the makeshift chair she'd erected for me at the Randwick training track. Gradually calming down, I fingered the icon reverently. I only wish my long-dead dad, whose life revolved around horses and the racetrack, could have sat beside me to soak it all up. Meanwhile, Gai carried on, barely noticing my agitation and never taking her gaze from her precious equine charges for long. It was quite an experience, hearing her expound on her unusual formation as apprentice to her famous dad, the legendary T. J. 'Tommy' Smith, amid the frequent, shouted instructions to her staff as they exercised the horses. 'Take him round again, Dave. He needs to work quite a bit harder.' And (to another assistant, Tania), 'Don't let that filly think she can behave like that. Just settle her down.'

Here was a female leader without peer in Australia—or elsewhere, for that matter. She inherited a mantle of skills from her legendary father, and then had to metamorphose into her own brand under the pressure of constant measurement against her father.

There is nothing so ruthlessly public as the finish of a horserace. Winning and losing are there for all to see. Gai's is a high-wire act, in which she is the main star, and we experience the spectacle of her winning and losing almost as a proxy for our own dreams. What interested me was how she viewed her authority as head of a business operation. What was her philosophy for employing staff, managing clients, keeping herself in her skin? I wanted an insight into a most distinctive form of leadership.

Gai had invited me to join her for a mid-week working lunch, weekends being far too busy. Would I mind coming to the pool at Randwick? (She liked to supervise the horses' swimming, a vital part of their preparation.) There wasn't much option as her schedule was so heavy, but I was delighted by the chosen venue. Having grown up around racetracks and trainers, I was terribly keen to watch her in action with both horses and staff. She employs between ninety and one hundred people from a mixed pool of talents. Her assistant, Steve, set up a table in the top paddock, replete with nice cloth and cutlery, and delivered plates of delicious sandwiches. The trusty chauffeur, Damien, was, as ever, hovering close by, judging whether or not an umbrella was necessary to shield us from the blazing sun. The car, as Gai says, is her office. Damien was brought on board as driver early in the 2000s because her increasing tiredness was threatening to cause a major accident. Now, they tear around the place 'like Batman and Robin', and Gai has regained her chutzpah after a distinct period of ennui—not that most of us in the crowd noticed anything. But she did. She is acutely aware of the levels of enthusiasm required as captain of the venerable Tulloch Lodge stables, which she has built into the conglomerate, Gai Waterhouse Racing.

> Gai: I have clients who are white-collar workers and staff who are no-collar workers. I have every possible category of person working for me: six to twelve different types of workers, with every manner of skills. And I have to make all the groups work together well. It's all so much about managing people, and you learn from every experience. Whatever happens makes things a bit easier the next time. But I make it clear: it's my way or the highway. Definitely my way or the highway!
>
> Geraldine: Do you welcome people who might argue with you or give you feedback that might be a bit tough to hear?
>
> Gai: Oh, if they were to tell me that I am doing the wrong thing with the horses, or if they have a different view about the horses, I will accept that. I will listen. I did it just the other day. Somebody said that they didn't think I was going about things the right way and I accept that. I most definitely will listen to feedback. But there's no doubt, it's my way that matters.

In other interviews, she has expanded on this, saying the horses are the 'easy-peasy part'. When problems emerge she can usually fix them or the lack of a solution becomes obvious. Good horse-people can't be clock-watchers, she says, because 'the thoroughbred has no sense of time'. Her ninety or so staff, who she regards as quasi-family, bowl up to work with a wondrous range of human foibles alongside their skills: the 'multi-lingual, multi-sexual, multi-everything' qualities that make the racing industry such a special case. *She* is a special case, which is obvious to all. Maybe this partly explains why her capacity to be a model for other women has barely been explored. Gai definitely bridges what you might call 'old Australia' and the very contemporary Australian entertainment/hospitality sector into which racing fits. The older version is vivid for millions of us, exemplified by the familiar routine of race day, race callers and the related Runyonesque hierarchies and eccentricities: jockeys, strappers, bookies, the animals themselves. And while strong elements of that older heritage remain, modern racing must also compete for market share within a highly competitive sector. It is a mighty challenge, which the industry acknowledges and which Gai internalises deeply. She takes her responsibilities incredibly seriously. She crafts her message till it is exactly right, and then combines it with intense discipline and a somewhat dispassionate approach to her business. Dispassionate, I hear you say? Surely not. Isn't she the one with the amazing hats, the huge smile and the fever-pitch excitement up in the stands when one of her charges storms up the straight? That is indeed Gai. And while I wouldn't say that all this feeling is bogus, I suspect it is a performance, in significant ways. Like any good CEO trying to promote a company image and beat off rivals, her behaviour is planned and systematic.

Gai: I really do like fashion and style, but really it's about the glamour of racing. I think that's what I try to project, the glamour of it. I think it's a very important part of my business, part of my whole approach. I'm promoting the trappings of racing: all the excitement and the fun and the drama that people can experience.

Geraldine: In some ways, it's a very old-fashioned industry, isn't it?

Gai: Absolutely. It hasn't changed a bit. It's pathetic really, but that's how it is. People have got to be able to work with me, and I have to be able to work with them. If things go wrong, I wipe them out of my mind. Things happen, and I don't dwell on them. That's what my father was like, completely future-orientated. My mother would ask questions about going back over something and he'd say, no, no, we're not going to do that, we're looking forward. It's a huge operation you know. A big lot of people. It's complicated.

Geraldine: Do you think work has taken up too much of your life? Is there any sense of balance there?

Gai: Oh, it has been too time-consuming. There have been huge costs. It has really been quite sad what I haven't been able to do. I think people think, oh, she's won the Golden Slipper and the Melbourne Cup in the one year, she must be made of money. But it's not like that. There are tremendous costs in our industry. You don't make lots of money. But it was the life I chose and that's fine.

Geraldine: What about friendships?

Gai: Oh, look, I keep friends, those who can fit in with my lifestyle. Basically that's got to happen.

Fitting in means accommodating the incredible discipline involved in all horse-trainers' lives. Gai's alarm rings six mornings a week at 2.30 am. She's at the track by 3 am, with the first ride an hour later. She has said on her blog, 'In My Words', that her energy springs from 'living a quiet life, eating well, having a daily massage, where she succumbs to any tiredness, sleeping during the day, maintaining routines and 9.30 pm to bed'. Comments about her from clients and race-men frequently stress her boundless energy, though that's not what I see. In fact, she presents as rather self-contained and focused, rather than exuberantly extrovert.

I remember noting right after her triumph in 2013, when Fiorente won the Melbourne Cup, that she seemed a titch disconnected on television, somewhat bemused by all the joy around her, but not joyous from *within*. Maybe her dreams had come finally true, I wondered to myself, bringing that accompanying feeling of anticlimax. Perhaps the disciplined nature of the quest had leeched out much of the ecstasy. Or maybe it was so epic that she kept it private just for once. Maybe the best celebrations were behind closed doors with her children and 'real rock, Rob', her husband. I didn't get a chance to ask her during our conversation, because other quirky gems popped out. Sit with Gabriel Marie Waterhouse (nee Smith) for even a short time (about forty-five minutes, in this instance) and her trademark candour will reveal views guaranteed to shock a modern female sensibility. Yes, she can make your jaw drop. She is her own creation.

Geraldine: Do you think of yourself as a woman achieving in the workplace? A woman who has risen to this position of leadership?

Gai: I don't think of myself like that. I don't think of my sex in the workplace at all, not at all. I think it is a real disadvantage, in fact, to think like that. I think a lot of young women are a real worry. Have you ever seen such a bunch of disappointed, unhappy people as a lot of young modern women? I mean, after all, what do you need? You need a family, you need a man and you need work. And they seem to be dissatisfied on all three counts

Geraldine: What about the business of bringing young women into your company, of developing them?

Gai: Young women today are at a real disadvantage, compared with when I went through. Because there are far too many single women. Women have real 'attitude' these days and big chips on their shoulders. Call me old-fashioned, but I think that for all women, in all age groups, there are some verities and you have to know about them, you have to know where you sit. You've got to take some things on the chin. It's important that young people keep open minds on things. No one just cops it any more. They just don't seem to know how to take a setback and get on with it.

Geraldine: Where are the women jockeys or trainers, especially the trainers?

Gai: They don't exist! It's too hard. It can't be done. Look at the jockeys: we could have had lots more female jockeys. They're not there. They vanish. They come in and then they vanish. On young women trainers: there's no hope, because the costs are just too great. You need to be training with BMWs and Mercedes [in terms of horseflesh] to make it, not just to have a few horses here and there. You've got absolutely no chance. The related labour costs are far too high. But I utterly accept it's a man's world. Of course it's a man's world. We all know that.

Geraldine: How do you handle the alpha males around you? I know you've dealt with a few: we've seen you do so on television.

Gai: I love alpha males. They're the most vulnerable of all. My business is all about alpha males: horses and men. I am very intuitive about what a man wants and needs. My job is to work that out and then deliver it. I go with the flow, but I am paid not to aggravate them.

Geraldine: But do you ever stand up for yourself with them? Do you stand your ground?

Gai: Oh yes, but a lot of the time, I just go with the flow. I don't take them on. That's my strength. Women have to work out what the men want and then basically know how to deliver that and get on with it. That's always been the case.

You'd have to thoroughly enjoy your work to endure the public gaze that accompanies racing. *Sydney Morning Herald* racing writer Chris Roots summarised it pithily in his December 2013 Year In Review, under the headline, 'Story of the Year': 'It was the best of years. It was the worst of years. Gai Waterhouse could have borrowed from the start of Charles Dickens' *Tale of Two Cities* to describe her 2013.' Indeed that seems an apt allusion. The list of Gai's successes over the previous twelve months was impressive. One of her recent champions Pierro, which she described as possibly the best horse she'd ever trained, had won both the Canterbury Stakes and the George Ryder Stakes, adding to his prestigious triple crown win as a two-year-old. He was then promptly sold to stud for more than $30 million. Another of her charges, Overreach, won the Slipper, and there was Fiorente's Melbourne Cup victory in November. However, the nadir of her year was surely the very public row that started at Randwick on 27 April, which would, as Roots described it, 'put racing on the front pages, end a friendship and have Waterhouse fighting hard for her family name'. Prominent businessman, horse owner and long-time Tulloch Lodge client John Singleton alleged before the race on television that his well-regarded mare, More Joyous, was 'off'. His suspicions appeared to be borne out when she subsequently ran second last in the All Aged Stakes. What so angered Singleton was that Gai's bookmaking son, Tom, was heard telling his mates pre-race that the horse could not win due to a small health setback. This can occur to these highly trained animals but trainers are obliged to inform the racing stewards immediately, to ensure full transparency.

Gai's equipoise most definitely deserted her throughout this two-week saga. It was a sensational yarn if ever there was one. I think it was the first time I had really seen her angry and discombobulated. 'It's an absolute disgrace,' she said of Singleton, a former big client. 'He has brought racing into disrepute.' Let the record show, however, that while Singleton was fined $15,000 by the stewards, his allegations regarding More Joyous were confirmed when Gai was also fined $7000 for not reporting conditions that could have affected the horse's performance in the lead-up to a race.

Old T. J. 'Tommy' Smith would probably have told her to just move on, look ahead, not back. And there is no doubt that she would have listened. She had plenty of practice while he was alive and his spirit clearly dwells deep inside her. She is in awe of him, simple as that, which could be a double-edged sword. Racing idealises legends like Tommy Smith. So even if she wanted to, Gai could never really escape working beside a ghost. It is hardly liberating. However, she ushered in the twenty-first century with her own brand of achievement, training the first, second and third placegetters in the Slipper in 2001, and two years later equalling her father's Sydney training record with 156 wins.

Gai: Dad was absolutely critical. He was just the best. He was the master of his game and I learned everything from him. I thought so much of his talents. I was an only child. I spent an enormous amount of time with him, and he was an extremely powerful influence. The nuns were also a very big influence on me at Kincoppal in Rose Bay, but, really, my father was the one who was the key. I was constantly talking to him, constantly watching him. I heard him talking to his clients. I saw it all and I took in everything associated with him.

Geraldine: What about your mother, whom I've seen you with at functions? I felt you got along very well. Surely she was an influence.

Gai: Yes, my mother had a very big influence on me. She, I think, gave me all my style, such that I have. Mum used to say that she spent all her life being Tommy's wife and then, when he died, she spent all her life being Gai's mother. We were very close. Basically she gave Dad all the polish, all the knowledge, all the rounding out that he didn't have. She was terribly important, but really it was my father who was the huge influence on me.

Looking at the Smith household, through the lens of a similar Irish-Catholic racing household on the other side of Australia, I have always had some sympathy for Gai. We both had memorable fathers, though mine was nothing like as dominating as hers. Mine, Gerry, thought T. J. was a champion, though he assumed he was a tough bastard, as the Irish could be: not the sort to give lots of praise, I'd bet.

> Gai: No, he wasn't big on the praise. He certainly knew how to criticise, but he gave me lots of help.
>
> Geraldine: Did he consciously groom you, do you think?
>
> Gai: Yes, he did. It was not just a job, you know. It was a way of life—that's what he transmitted to me. It was an absolute way of life.

There is one lovely quote I turned up from an interview T. J. gave to racing writer Grant Vandenberg in 1997. Would Gai make a good trainer, the grand old man was asked? 'She's good at anything, especially when it comes to horses. She's got a good eye for a horse and is a real horse lover and has everything it takes to make a trainer.' I wonder if he ever said that, directly, to his daughter.

Interestingly, Gai believes her training as an actor was important to the position she now holds. After completing a bachelor of arts at the University of New South Wales in 1975, she modelled for a while, then acted in the Australian television drama *The Young Doctors*. Then, in the UK, her work included *Doctor Who* episodes and some theatre roles. It all contributed to a readiness for performance as a central part of her public persona, which in turn underpins her business.

> Gai: I think my time in the theatre really did help quite a bit. It taught me to believe in myself. It also really honed my presenting skills. It helped me learn about the business of how I was going to look and present myself. And of course I very much enjoyed it. I did learn to be very tough though too, in terms of taking on pressure. I had to make

> that decision. For instance, when I was there with Tom Baker, he'd have this huge go at me, and I could have either burst into tears or toughened up. So I toughened up.

Gai Waterhouse pays quite a high price for her public success. And she's willing to do so, for now anyway. Day in day out, she lives by the dictates of an oppressive schedule. But without it, she believes she'd forfeit the way of life bequeathed by her beloved father. And she lives in a family with a special talent for making the headlines—and not necessarily positive ones. Yet she clearly thrives within these settings and sees them as her sanctuary, even when many others wonder how she takes it all.

She's known for picking good horses and making them win and for making racing fun—a valuable set of assets. Horse owner John McDonnell told *Gai's Gazette*—all part of the marketing—that 'she is the most incredibly positive person I have ever met…she is really capable of making a silk purse out of a sow's ear'. As her influence as a racing leader has grown, has she evolved? Has the success produced some alchemy from within the woman herself? Has she prised more respect out of her community? Which inspires which? Clearly, for Gai, she has. She has learned to win—first in her basic skill of training horses, and then in turning that into a good business that pays wages each week. What a pity, though, that she sees such little hope for more women to break through in her world. I have to confess that such fatalism from this dynamo left me full of dismay.

CHAPTER 8

NANCY MILNE

The Rule of Law

Nancy Milne OAM had planned to be a journalist but eventually chose a career in the law. She has spent her professional life in various prominent firms where she garnered considerable respect as a commercial litigator, working on professional negligence and directors' liability cases and some prominent insurance coverage disputes. She has worked on federal government policy review panels, and was a consultant with the law firm Clayton Utz until 2012. Nancy donates considerable time to several not-for-profit organisations and sits on leading commercial boards.

ONE obvious measure of readiness for leadership is the capacity to handle pressure: sudden, intense drama and relentless slow-building pressure. Nancy Milne is accustomed to both. In her almost-forty-year career as a corporate lawyer and non-executive director of not-for-profit and for-profit firms, she has known the shock of discovering that everything she thought was settled was anything but.

On one occasion, back in 2003, she was only three weeks into a new chairmanship of the local subsidiary of a big insurance company, her first at this level, when she became aware of some significant irregularities in one area of its operation. Furthermore, the extent of the problem was unclear. How much did the European head office know? How easily could it be fixed? But, more importantly, should the regulator, the Australian Prudential Regulatory Authority (APRA), be alerted? If this route was taken, there would be no turning back. Once the regulator is 'inside the walls', the whole relationship between it and the company shifts. Then and now, APRA constantly exhorts companies in these vital areas of insurance, banking and superannuation to forewarn them of any potential difficulties. It says the intent is to help rather than scold. But many within the industry are lukewarm at best about opening the door to the policeman when things could be messy. The glittering standard of transparency can be hard to adhere to when the going gets tough.

Discussion at the company's executive levels and in the boardroom was intense. All Nancy's instincts told her to bring APRA in. But she was the newbie. And while there was support for her view from other independent directors and the firm's general counsel, other advisers bitterly opposed the strategy. The stakes were high in terms of company reputation. Naturally, that reputation depends on squeaky-clean operations in its custodianship of trillions of dollars of other people's investments.

Eventually, after judicious consultation with trusted advisers and the company's legal team, Nancy made a captain's call. Overriding the wishes of some of her colleagues and amid the threat of legal injunctions, she advocated picking up the phone to APRA. She has never regretted her actions. The problem in the company was serious, but it was isolated within a relatively short time, and resolved.

Crucially, Nancy dealt with all this acute stress on top of her day jobs. Those sayings—'if you want something done, give it to a busy person' and 'everything comes at once'—were never truer than during Nancy Milne's baptism of fire as chair. A copybook test of leadership, it required agile, cool-headed resilience in the face of unforeseen challenges. Above all, it required an ethical sensibility. There was, at heart, a basic question to be considered: what is the right thing to do? There doesn't seem much doubt that her judgment and temperament proved equal to the task. But the experience took its toll. And it taught her a crucial lesson about the need to move outside her comfort zone.

Nancy: Yes, I was at Clayton Utz. It was also happening at the same time as the special commission of enquiry into James Hardie [the asbestos firm], where I was acting for the underfunded trust established by Hardies to take on all its asbestos claims. I had so much on my plate. I was also chairing the review of insurance legislation with Alan Cameron for the government. In the dramas at the insurance company, after APRA was called in, there was some criticism from within the organisation: all you are doing is looking after your own skin and is that in the best interest of the organisation? I was lucky to have independent directors who supported me, and so there were initially three of us who secured an agreement to go to the regulator and provide it with some information. I was subsequently criticised for having gone beyond the proper bounds.

Geraldine: Was it in your remit to do that? Did you have to seek head-office approval?

Nancy: I had to seek permission. I had to get advice. I went to see Tom Bathurst, who's now Chief Justice of New South Wales. He was a QC at the time and he was fabulous. I tried to ring the CEO, and, for whatever reason, he wasn't there or didn't take my call and the General Counsel from the global group rang me. It was a very tense time.

Geraldine: I can imagine. What were your insides doing?

Nancy: I felt sick. Physically ill. I also thought, well you know, my reputation…

Geraldine: Could be shredded?

Nancy: Gone! And there was a huge amount of resistance within the company. Some people disagreed with everything I was doing and were very hostile. Anyway, I managed to get agreement to go to the regulator [APRA], who was fantastic.

Geraldine: Was it after this that you got breast cancer?

Nancy: I had the first lot of breast cancer before that, and then I got a second lot in 2007.

Geraldine: Do you ever wonder?

Nancy: I do wonder. I do wonder, but I've talked to my oncologist about it and he says stress is stress and we don't know its full impact. The whole episode at the company and all the related drama was probably the most stressful thing I've ever been involved in. I have been involved in some subsequently too, but that was the most stressful.

Geraldine: And it triggered some changes, didn't it, in your decision-making, about the time and energy you give to things?

Nancy: I think I decided that I really didn't want to work those kinds of hours. I had probably already decided that after my first bout of breast cancer, but this incident with the company and APRA really reinforced it! It's the old Nietzchean thing: if you survive these kinds of times you grow stronger. I think I had been tough before, but I probably got tougher.

Geraldine: Still, you did come to an appreciation of limits though? That's the impression I got.

Nancy: That's exactly right. I did think it was huge. I'd been in the firestorm, to use the current analogy. I really had been in the firestorm on that one.

Geraldine: How do you bring people along with you at times like this?

Nancy: I think that's really hard and was probably the thing we [the independent directors and I] didn't do as well as we could have in that situation. We had a huge issue, with a lot of work streams that had to be addressed. We had confidentiality imposed on us too.

Geraldine: So you couldn't even share all this?

Nancy: At the end of it we were criticised for not having engaged with the broader members of the executive team, and it was fair criticism. We later went back and we did a kind of analysis and debrief of everything that had happened. There were still very different views about how we might handle something like that in the future. I don't know, if I was in that kind situation again I would…

Geraldine: Do things differently?

Nancy: I probably would, being conscious now of that deficiency. I am not quite sure how, but the key is that you have got to surround yourself with good people and maybe take more of a multi-disciplinary approach, rather than letting it be handled by the legal team, which seemed sensible at the time, given that it was a regulatory issue. And probably because of my legal background, I tended to give priority to the legal side because I was familiar with it—I could understand it.

Nancy Milne originally considered a career in journalism. But her parents, both with experience in the Fourth Estate, wouldn't hear of it, 'under no circumstances'. They wanted something more solid for her. So, after dismissing diplomacy, Nancy chose law by a process of elimination, though she now seems a natural. She entered a profession with an established body of knowledge, built brick by brick, where apprenticeships are served using explicit tools of trade and manuals of experience laden with precedent. The student knows she must crawl before she can walk, that she must steadily accumulate knowledge and retrace the sacred ground of forebears who've tested and retested the tenets that underpin our community.

This seems to me a very solid foundation for authority. I sense that women with explicit professional credentials derive a great deal of confidence from them, more so than is generally acknowledged. Whether it helps them move from one area of expertise to another, however, is the question, as Nancy discovered when she made the transition to board director and had to tap into a new set of skills. Working on boards or for the peak bodies or committees of review that senior women are asked to join, introduces women to arenas that are outside their normal range. A more diffuse mix of skills is invariably required too, including influence peddling and positioning, which may not have been prized in their original professional jobs.

Although I was never attracted to it, I can now see how the law provides a woman with a good base for broader commitments outside her professional expertise, as well as being a richly rewarding career for someone who is good at it. And, clearly, Nancy was good at it, right from the outset. She was given a set of riding instructions from a highly respected woman, former chief judge of the Land and Environment Court, the late Mahla

Pearlman (the first female head of the New South Wales Law Society). Judge Pearlman was passionate about good lawyers being those who problem solved rather than merely identified the problem for the client. Nancy took her advice to heart. She is proud of her work; she believes that it can deliver for the broader good. The privilege of mattering has always been a great motivator for Nancy. She is also highly competitive and never afraid of hard work. During one intense period, when she was engaged for three years helping to sort out the collapse of the Occidental and Regal Insurance Group in the early 1990s, the pressure was relentless. She was appointed towards the end of 1990, and the only day she took off was Christmas Day.

> Nancy: There was so much happening. It was a situation where I really had to develop juggling skills, in terms of trying to work out what the priorities were and, with a huge team of people, who was doing what, how we were going to get to where we needed to be. I don't think I had any formal training for the pressure and complexity, but you learn on the job. There is a toughness you develop, and you do become quite thick-skinned and quite determined. Your mental ability too, I think, develops and it comes back to some of the things that Mahla taught me. It was about picking out what was important, not sweating the small stuff, I suppose. But the toughness was critical.

Nancy's willingness to accept the rigours of high-level work demands was brought home to me firsthand at the start of a Milford Track walk for my fiftieth birthday. Nancy and her husband, Graham Fox, joined me and a group of friends to walk the legendary New Zealand track. The trek had been planned for months. Winter was about to close in and we were booked on the second-last tour of the season. There was no rescheduling possible. There we were, nervous and excited, having flown in from various parts of the globe to meet at a particular hiking shop in nearby Queenstown where we'd kit ourselves out and set off to 'leave civilisation' for four days. Nancy and her husband were a bit late. Then Graham arrived to announce that he *thought* Nancy would be okay to come on the walk, but that something had suddenly emerged at the office. It was pretty big and she just may not be able to do the walk because she needed to be near a phone! We were all stunned. Could it possibly be that serious? Well, yes. It related to key people within her firm's partnership, and her advice could be critical over the next little while. So, for a few hours, the rest of us waited expectantly, on the fringes of highly charged phone calls. Eventually, with some apprehension, Nancy decided that matters were sufficiently in hand for her to sally forth into the New Zealand wilderness, though she did set up fallback positions with the walk organisers.

Nancy's strong work ethic has established her an equally strong reputation among her peers, where her cool judgment is keenly sought. But as the years have progressed, it has also left a legacy of some guilt—the infamous monkey on a working woman's back—though maybe, in Nancy's case, less so than the horror stories suggest. It is there, no doubt about it, but Nancy isn't crushed by admitting she carries guilt. Neither is she serene about its long-term impact.

Nancy: There was a job to be done, and I was the person who had to do it. I guess the other side of that is I kept being brought back down to earth because I do have a family and have children [two sons]. I was spending a lot of time in Melbourne over one period. I was away from home and Graham really kept the home fires burning, as did Betty [their live-in housekeeper]. I missed the boys desperately, but I also took a view at the time that when I was going to be at home I wasn't going to do anything like housework. If the house was a mess that was fine. I would try to get some quality time with the kids, things like going away on holidays. I would never have dreamt of going away without the boys; that just wasn't negotiable.

Geraldine: Were you conscious of a time when you decided to fulfil all your career potential, and possibly take on a leadership position, even if that meant that some of your family duties took a secondary role?

Nancy: Well, during that big job that took me to Melbourne, I felt a huge amount of guilt. But I had to get the job done, and I also thought, I've probably got the dream legal job given my experience and qualifications and everything else. I've got the job of a lifetime and I've got to do this properly. Because we were looking after ordinary people who were the ones who were going to suffer if this didn't go right, and that's always been quite a driving force for me.

Geraldine: Did the boys ever say anything to you or, for that matter, did Graham? Do you have any memories of someone saying, that's enough, or I'm sick of it?

Nancy: No, no, I think the boys just accepted it. We were incredibly lucky that we had a wonderful live-in housekeeper who had been there for a long time who was a member of the family. I talked to them about this much later on and they said, it was never a problem, Mum. Why did you worry about us?

So with all this hard experience and acquired wisdom behind her, surely she didn't feel any of the so-called imposter syndrome said to dog rising women? Not as a lawyer, she immediately replied, but definitely as a director. It was about ten years ago, just as she'd reached a 'nice, sweet spot' in her legal career, that she stepped off the proverbial cliff into non-executive director land, which led her to her insurance firestorm. She discovered she was in foreign territory. Also, she had to disprove some preconceptions about herself. She believes there is a real perception within the business sector that lawyers don't make very good directors because they don't think big picture or have finance skills, an accounting background or commercial line management experience. Nevertheless she took up the offer of board work because her competitive spirit was sparked and she wanted to start preparing the ground to reposition herself, at some point, away from the long, long hours involved in being a senior legal partner. She wanted to sample a new professional world using her legal skills, about which she remained fully confident.

Nancy's observations about the vagaries of board life intrigued me. Australian women's representation on big company boards, at sixteen per cent in the Top 100 firms, is lamentably low. About once a month, this kind of statistic makes headlines, accompanied by predictable indignation about the glacial pace of change and the usual analysis. It prompted action late in 2013 from an uber-powerful group of CEOs calling themselves Champions of Change. They set themselves the target of imprinting the issue of women's leadership on the national agenda. And they've boldly aimed to have female directors making up fifty per cent of the significant boards by 2020.[8] The group has committed considerable personal energy and resources to this new venture. All the literature on this subject suggests gender ratios change significantly only when chief executives become involved, rather than when it is left to middle management. So this high level Champions group projects an image of more seriousness than previous efforts. But I wonder if they've incorporated the wisdom on offer from experienced practitioners like Nancy. It might change their view of the challenge ahead.

Nancy: If someone comes to me with a legal problem in my area, I am confident that I can deal with it. But, as a director, I think that you are drawing on different skills and need a different approach. The other thing I find is that so often it's hard to get a word in at board level, really hard. I take a view that if I don't have anything new to contribute I'm not going to jump in and say something. I don't know that some of the men share that view.

Geraldine: But, by the sound of it from the numbers of boards you are invited to join, it hasn't done your reputation any harm.

Nancy: No, and you often hear it said that the greatest affirmation of somebody as a director is that when they say something it's worth consideration, and that's what I try to do. But there are situations where I can go to a meeting and I feel quite frustrated that I haven't made a substantial contribution. And then I go and agonise over that, and I do agonise over it.

Geraldine: Still?

Nancy: Still. Yeah. But there's a really interesting development.

A lot of women now are getting together and talking about those kinds of things and helping each other. I'm involved with a couple of those groups. It's really quite wonderful to see this kind of just blossoming. It's a sort of grassroots thing.

Geraldine: But what's the difference for men on these boards?

Nancy: Interestingly at the moment the men are all complaining. The whingers are fantastic! They say, I am being discriminated against because I don't wear a skirt; it is much harder for me to get a board role because everyone is trying to appoint women.

And surely this is good news. But after years of effort to increase the numbers of women on boards, here and elsewhere, why is the percentage still so low? Why would this particular arena of enterprise be so impervious to change? Having sat on seven boards—not-for-profit boards like the St James Ethics Centre, a Department of Foreign Affairs–related entity, the Australia-Malaysia Institute, a religious-order hospital and one commercial entity during the 1990s—I have given this a lot of thought. In fact, the rules and mores of the boardroom are quite baroque, but no one says that out loud. They are not like those that dominate an average working life. For instance, they're certainly different from the formalities associated with editorial meetings, which I'm used to. These gatherings are much more democratic, more task-orientated and practical. In the meetings of formal boards, there is a lot of etiquette and hierarchy—much more than is found in the flatter organisational style of today's working world. When I joined boards in the late 1980s, I was quite surprised by the codes of conduct that I encountered. And I don't think

I'm alone, having talked to other women and men on boards. Aggression or frustration is allowed, but within fairly strict limits. For example, speaking via the chair must be observed: 'through you Mr Chair, or Madame Chair, could I suggest we send this report back to be redrafted please?' (Translation: this is a piece of obfuscating rubbish.) The formality is upheld by all but powerful men, several of whom I have seen break all the rules. Much negotiating is done before meetings, especially during turbulent times, which took me quite a while to work out. I simply bowled up, thinking everything was on the table for discussion, whereas it most certainly was not. The conundrum is this: if you're a woman and have been invited onto these boards, generally speaking, you'll have advanced to senior levels within modern workplaces. Then, suddenly, you're thrown back into a forum that can feel rule-bound and opaque. Not all boards are like this, but arriving at one unprepared, and then having to learn its strange ways, as well as the complexities of the business entity, is a real challenge.

Nancy: I know. For instance, the last thing I want to do is to sound shrill if I'm trying to make a point.

Geraldine: What's the matter with sounding shrill?

Nancy: Well, I just don't think it is a good look. You lose some of your authority. Women tend to do that, men don't.

Geraldine: Would you have worried about this in the law? Are you really talking about the presentation of your argument, about your voice level and management of emotions?

Nancy: I think it is really important. One thing I did learn in the law was that, in terms of advocacy, there were very few occasions where an aggressive, bombastic approach achieved much at all. In fact, one of the best pieces of advice I was ever given was to avoid adjectives. It's interesting how much more forceful an argument can become when you make it very simple and compelling in a very considered and reasonable way rather than thumping the table.

Geraldine: But, what if you meet resistance?

Nancy: If you meet resistance, that's a problem. Where do you go? I mean all that you can do is say, look, I just want to raise this point.

Geraldine: Have you watched other women on boards? Do you see a pattern of mistakes they make?

Nancy: I haven't observed a lot of mistakes, but there are a lot of directors' functions I go to and I watch some women say things that I think are misguided. It's actually interesting to see those people over time, because generally they do mature and they do become less outspoken.

Geraldine: It sounds to me as if the women who are thriving on boards don't take big risks with personality?

Nancy: That's right. They don't take big risks with personality. I think the men probably do.

Geraldine: Maybe the range of female expression allowed on boards right now is still narrower than it is for men, and maybe boards are inherently pretty conservative places?

Nancy: Very, very. And I would be very, very careful on most of my boards—I wouldn't ever reveal a strong political view. I would talk about my home life only occasionally, not a great deal, maybe I'd talk about music and art and things like that. A lot of the men will talk about sport.

> We're talking about questions of tone here and general social chat. Women do have to be a little bit careful about not being seen as too soft and fluffy. In terms of business diversity, when there is one woman on a board, it's such a struggle, and then you get two and there's an exponential lift in discussion all round. All the studies are now saying that the more women there are on boards the better the results. No one is giving a scientific reason for that, but my guess is that it means things are a bit more focused on people and culture within the business, those kinds of things.

Working through the ranks to attain these enviable levels of influence is heavily reliant on a good education. These days it is probably taken for granted and, therefore, not identified as a critical value. Regrettably, among some groups it may even be less prized now than in former times. For Nancy, education was an unqualified public and private good in her own life, and she remains passionate about it. It spurs her towards her pro bono work for the Montessori movement and the Good Beginnings NGO.

It was a pleasure, as well, to hear her nominate three key female influences in her life. Most of my interviewees talked about strong male figures in their lives, especially engaged, committed fathers. However Nancy's mother, Margaret, who died tragically at the age of fifty-eight, left a powerful legacy, of both positive and negative memories. This 'highly intelligent woman' effectively stopped work after Nancy's birth, leading to extraordinary frustration and suffering over the years. But this brought about a ferocious commitment in Margaret to educate Nancy so that she wouldn't endure the same fate. There was Justice Mahla Pearlman, and, indirectly, the influence of the legendary educationalist Betty Archdale, who, as principal of North Shore Sydney school Abbotsleigh School for Girls (1958–70), turned it into one of the city's best intellectual cauldrons and a magnet for ambitious parents. Nancy's mother was determined: her daughter was set for Abbotsleigh, and Nancy won one of the school's scholarships.

Nancy: I think I was lucky in that, from a very early age, I was quite bright, and in that I had formative people in my life. I had some teachers who singled me out, in fact, one teacher in particular. When I was in fourth class she said, I think you should skip fifth class and go straight to sixth class, and you also need to do some extra stuff. She started me learning French when I was in fourth class. I didn't realise at that point the significance of all of that.

Geraldine: Starting a sense of self-belief?

Nancy: Yeah. I was pretty competitive and it was very important to me. I'm so embarrassed about all of this now. It was very important to me to be right up there at the top of the class. So I was delighted when I went into sixth class, then was Dux, having skipped fifth.

Geraldine: Did you imagine this was where you'd be in your life, that it would take you here?

Nancy: No, no, I didn't at all. I thought a lot of it was more luck than anything else. I had this view that I was a lucky young woman. Most people didn't have the quality of the education that I did, and I really think that is such a critical thing for everybody. Because there was an absolute, fundamental belief that all of us would go on to university and that we could do anything we wanted to do. A

> lot of that was to do with Betty Archdale, an extraordinary person. When we got out of school and went to university, we suddenly realised, or I certainly did, that it wasn't plain sailing, as I'd been led to believe. It was not only a different environment, because you were going into a male and female situation, but also so much tougher than I had anticipated.

As it turned out, Nancy was well equipped for tough environments and for leading others through them. She says she never stops learning and I believe she means it. Without that background of legal skills, would she have found herself in leadership roles? Possibly not, although her competitiveness and adaptability would have asserted themselves in whatever she did. Plus there is her capacity for judgment. When Nancy proffers a professional opinion, you are wise to listen. She won't insist you hear: that's not her style. But you're a mug if you ignore her.

CHAPTER 9

SANDRA HARDING

Born to Rule

Professor Sandra Harding grew up in a forces family that was determined to offer her the best educational chances possible for a bright young woman. Armed with an honours degree in science, she went on to train as an economic sociologist here and in the US, developing a strong interest in research into organisational methods. Academic research, publications and leadership positions are dotted throughout her busy career in various universities and in her membership of public bodies—from the Queensland Commission of Audit to director of the North Queensland Cowboys Rugby League Club, to the University Grants Commission. Sandra is now vice-chancellor and president of James Cook University in Townsville and is chair of the peak body Universities Australia.

IN a university job interview during the 1980s, eager twenty-something-year-old would-be lecturer Sandra Harding was asked whether she intended to have children. Clearly her employment rested on her answer, and that outraged her. None of their business, she thought. When she returned to work in her late twenties after her first child, a colleague said, oh Sandra, I thought you would have taken the easy option and stayed home. On another occasion around this time, she found out that discussions were afoot among senior university colleagues as to whether her husband 'would mind' if she had to travel to fulfil her work duties. That very day, she took off her wedding ring and has not worn it since. She is still happily married to that same husband, Kevin Harding, who is well used to just going with the flow, she says.

What Sandra didn't tell me outright, but I can guess underlies all these stories, was this: she was a pretty, petite blonde woman, about whom lots of wrong assumptions were made for a while. She was not seen as the ambitious type, as someone likely to prioritise work advancement over family obligations. If her interviewers had known how to draw out the real Sandra with their questions, they might have discovered a person uncannily well equipped for taking charge. The *Australian* newspaper summarised her abilities in March 2013, after she was appointed, unopposed, as chair of the peak body Universities Australia: 'She brings an impeccable track record, laudable independence and stylish chutzpah to the peak group. Harding will bring approachability, plain speaking and highly developed political skills to her role.'

Those qualities would not have necessarily been obvious at the time of those early interviews, in the 1980s, even to her. She was not a full-blown leader waiting to happen right there and then but her potential should have been obvious to perceptive superiors. It took one exceptional mentor and years of experience for her to discover how much she enjoyed management and that she had a flair for dealing with people. If the interviewers had been savvy enough to look beyond their stereotyped notions about this pretty, young girl-next-door in front of them, they might have discerned an unusual level of grit.

Sandra's background fortified her well for her many leadership roles of the last fifteen years. She springs from armed forces stock, and, as for most of the women I've interviewed, the kitchen-table lessons and the tone of the household were crucial elements in building the leader she has become. Her level-headed personality surely helps too. Virtually with her mother's milk, Sandra was introduced to the fundamental ethic that underpins military life: the concept of belonging to a group larger than the nuclear family, of living by a clear set of rules within a clear hierarchy, and of providing service to others.

She didn't actually use this word but my sense is that she believed it was a *virtuous* realm, one that prized fairness. It was worth striving to do your very best in life, and this was not merely an empty mantra. It was non-elite too. Sandra knows she can get along with a wide range of Australians. She went to Victorian primary and secondary state schools, in what she describes a 'most unsalubrious part of Melbourne'. She competed ferociously in neighbourhood softball and hockey competitions. And she has that lovely Australian middle-brow confidence about her place in the world. I could see neither envy nor smugness in her. Sandra is a classic product of a good family supported by an education system designed to equip people to tap their potential, no matter their parents' means. Back in Melbourne in the 1970s, she would never, ever have guessed that forty years later, she'd be judged North Queensland's Most Influential Person of 2013 by the Townsville *Bulletin* due to her work as vice-chancellor of James Cook University.

The trigger, in a way, was a conversation in the late 1970s with her adored father, Sydney, a warrant officer, on a Sunday night as they drove home from inner-city Footscray to Heidelberg past Melbourne University.

> Sandra: I remember looking at it and saying to my dad, who is this gorgeous man, I'm going to go there one day. And he said, well, if you can get in, we'll find a way to make that happen. It was just such a beautiful moment. And I think, in no small way, it enabled me. I knew I had my parents' confidence. I knew I had their support. And I knew I had their love.

Of course, the building blocks were laid earlier than that. Her father and mother were made aware as early as her grade four year that their little blonde poppet of a daughter had lots to offer.

Sandra: I went to Kingsville State School, with a lot of migrant children and a lot of people who went on to high school but then left very early. I did quite well at school and I remember years later my dad saying, I think it was at the end of grade five or grade four, that he came home after a parent–teacher interview where the teacher had said something along the lines of, you've got to understand she could do whatever she chooses. And that was sort of 'a moment'. Every now and then, he says to me, You know, I came home and I looked at you and thought, goodness me. And so there you are. But I never had any sense of that, I might say.

Geraldine: They weren't distracted by that? They just got on with rearing you?

Sandra: That's right. But I always used to start things. In primary school I started clubs; I liked being involved in things. If I saw something I'd do it as best as I could. Not quite so much in high school, I suppose. I was on the Student Representative Council—I was voted onto that—and I was vice captain in form one. I never had a sense that there was anything I couldn't do. I never had a sense that it was wrong of me to be thinking whatever I was thinking.

Geraldine: Even though your upbringing had a very orthodox structure, your mind was allowed to roam? You were encouraged by both parents?

Sandra: Yes. My father, like many of the best people in the military, is very accomplished. He is a very beautiful man with very high interpersonal skills. And he wasn't a senior person in the military either, just a regular sort of person. My mother could be quite formidable. She's also a wonderful person, and I can never remember a discouraging word from either of them, and certainly never from her. She trained as a mothercraft nurse initially, and even when my children were born or little, she never made any suggestion that what I was doing wasn't perfectly wonderful. She is fantastic, but she is the tough guy. My father used to call her the 'officer in charge'.

Geraldine: I noticed Paul Keating, in those television interviews with Kerry O'Brien, said his father was a sweet, lovely man and that his mother was a killer! I think the whole of Australia laughed.

Sandra: I know, well it was not dissimilar in my family. My mother is formidable. I have never actually said that to her, and I don't know how she would take it, quite frankly. But she was very much the disciplinarian; she was the one who was organised. And yet, when the time came for me to leave home, it was my father who was crushed, and my mother who said, you know, I understand. Because she had left Tasmania as a young woman and went on her own to Melbourne to be part of the bigger world. So she was brave, courageous and interesting, and polite and wonderful. She is a terrific person.

Geraldine: She could never be persuaded that her politeness was weakness, by the sound of it?

Sandra: No, no, no.

There has to be a direct link between her mother's brand of

politeness and one of Sandra's key insights about herself and her emphasis on good manners: 'I get along quite well with people, but every now and then I have to remind people not to confuse courtesy with weakness.' People who assume she will be a pushover, especially in union negotiations, can get a real shock. But one of Sandra's strengths is her ability to work with people, another area in which she believes she has been influenced by her father's career. Because in the military, she says, that cliché about people being an organisation's greatest asset really is critical. You have to trust your people and develop their strengths. Your life may depend on it.

Sandra is proud of her capacity to deal with conflict. I asked whether she had ever been accused of ruthlessness—that word that I believe strikes fear into the hearts of many women who might consider taking the helm of an organisation. What followed was an impressive manifesto for authority.

Sandra: That's a word [ruthless] that is fraught with emotion and meaning. To my mind, I can be absolutely decisive, crystal clear about why we are doing something and determined to do it, yes.

Geraldine: Even if you have to walk over people?

Sandra: I can't think of a time when I felt I walked over people. But that may not be others' perspective on it.

Geraldine: That's very important for your view of yourself, by the sound of it?

Sandra: It absolutely is. I think it is incredibly important that you face people. Whenever I've got an issue with anybody or something is going to happen, I will eyeball people. In the thick of the industrial relations business [involving a round of retrenchments] there was a part of the university that was very gung-ho and doing some things that, admittedly, were protected industrial action [under their industrial agreement], but it was very disruptive. And I came to the meeting and said, this is my perspective—it doesn't have to be your perspective, but I want you to know why I'm doing the things that I'm doing and why I think they're important, and I will leave you to make up your own mind. I don't try to convince people. It's not my job to do that, other than in subtle ways, I suppose. Anyway, I was applauded at the end of that meeting, and part of the discussion subsequently was: she didn't have to show up; she didn't have to do that. You have to be brave. You have to be a bit courageous and be there. I put my position, not in an apologetic sense, but in a clear unequivocal fashion. Again, I always say, it doesn't have to be your thinking, but it is important you understand why I am doing this.

Geraldine: But when people do test that courtesy of yours, what goes through your mind?

Sandra: I think I learned a lesson from my parents in this, certainly my father. I tend to get quieter, not noisier, and I think that brings the temperature down. I simply don't feed that sort of behaviour, and, during the industrial tensions that we had for a few months there, some things were being said that were not right, and I did say to a couple of people, you know that's not right; I'm really disappointed that you would do that when you know that it isn't right.

Geraldine: And they didn't do it again?

Sandra: Not that I saw. But who knows? I guess all I can do is put my view and be unequivocal about it. I think leaders have to be the best-behaved people. I absolutely fundamentally believe this. All of my emails will be 'Dear So and So', 'Cheers', 'Regards', 'Sincerely', whatever the case might be. If someone sends me something, I will send them something back. I follow the rules. If I don't follow the rules, why should anybody else? Even if they're not worthwhile—if they are our current rules, then either we change them or we all follow them. I feel very, very strongly about this. I know that if I came in to my office cranky about something—it could be nothing to do with work at all—I could put a whole lot of people off their job for the morning, because they will all spend part of their time wondering why I'm upset, or what I'm doing, or what has caused it and whose fault it was, or trying to flush out what it might be. That is self-indulgent behaviour. I can't do that to other people.

Those industrial tensions over a big cost-cutting exercise followed the Gillard government's surprise announcement about trimming university funding to redirect money to primary and secondary schools. This bombshell came just one week after Sandra took over the chairing role of Universities Australia. It was a baptism of fire, but Sandra proceeded with her usual methodical, calm sense of purpose.

Sandra believes she only says yes to invitations when her instincts tell her she is ready for whatever might be bowled up. Twice before in her career, she has declined what seemed like must-have positions because she felt underprepared. Even now, she feels she is quite young as a vice-chancellor and is a touch awed by her responsibilities as chair, considering the constant changes besetting the tertiary sector. So many have placed their trust in her methodical, calm readiness to accept responsibility for unforeseen events, like the big changes planned in the recent budget.

Extracting yourself, unscathed, from industrial strife in universities is never easy. The tug of war over conditions can easily claim the reputations of otherwise respected administrators. Sandra was aware of this, but not cowed by it. Early retirement was offered to certain academic staff in order to reduce numbers and save money. Almost simultaneously, details emerged publicly of considerably upgraded salaries for Sandra and other senior university staff. The *Courier-Mail* reported that despite a $26 million cut to JCU, Sandra's salary package had increased by twenty-nine per cent the previous year. Sandra explains that others decided the amount, not her, and that her salary is neither at the top nor the bottom of the range for Australian vice-chancellors; it was a periodic salary review designed to apply over the next five years and it reflected her increased level of responsibilities. But it certainly made the headlines in a way she would not have chosen. Though it doesn't seem to have particularly bothered her, because she felt it was just and within the rules.

There is another vital element to Sandra's commitment to leading others. She believes leadership ability resides in having a 'compelling idea about the world'. With it, she can then unambiguously say to others, this is not about me and my ego; it is about where we're *jointly* headed. In some management literature, this has been termed 'ternary leadership', that is, focusing on a third element beyond the predictable employer–employee binary kind. It is described as one of the key ways in which women (or any new arrivals to the scene) can assert themselves: immersing themselves in the mission of the organisation, plunging their talents, almost self-effacingly, into its wellbeing and growth.

Sandra lives out this leadership style via her bold plans for JCU to be recognised as Australia's 'University of the Tropics', an institution coordinating worldwide research in this vital region. Aristotle, she reminded me, wrote more than 2000 years ago about three zones of the world—the Frigid, the Temperate and the Torrid zones—insisting the only place where civilised human beings could live was the temperate. How wrong he was. Now containing forty per cent of the world's population and eighty per cent of its biodiversity, the tropics also hosts many of the world's critical issues. In the last three years, Sandra has instigated and led a major project on the state of the tropics involving a consortium of twelve international institutions. The project report is due soon, and she believes it will be transformative. What thrills her, makes her eyes sparkle, is that northern Australia—in conjunction with, say, Singapore—could become the site of fit-for-purpose solutions, ahead of traditional knowledge centres like London and Washington. Some of the African collaborators have already revelled in this possibility after their involvement. 'It's about, in no small way, aiming to change the way the world views itself,' Sandra says. It sounded like an extension of her earlier primary-school days of setting things up, I suggested.

Sandra had also been a driving force during the 1990s when she established the Business Dean's Council, while dean of business at Queensland University of Technology—her big step up in management. She had noticed that deans of science, law and other faculties met regularly, but not deans of business. So she set about addressing that.

Sandra: I thought to myself, goodness me, there's no voice of business education anywhere or economics for that matter. So I contacted all of my colleagues and said, look this is crazy; of course we compete—very, very strongly in many ways—but if there aren't things we can collaborate on, I will go he. And so, I invited everyone to what turned out to be the inaugural meeting. And it's still going today, which I am very pleased about. But again, it's a quiet pride, because there'll be people even within the business deans who wouldn't know what went into making it happen.

There was a pivotal mentor in Sandra's career whom she regularly cites in our conversation. He was a long-serving vice-chancellor at QUT, where Sandra worked prior to her move to JCU. She watched him care-fully and admired him a lot. He was a very humble individual, someone so focused on doing the best job, she couldn't see his ego getting in the way. He modelled self-awareness and the idea of highlighting the job to be done over the strategy to get there—attributes Sandra has never forgotten. How exactly did he contribute to Sandra's evolution from the young woman who had seriously considered becoming a flight attendant into an assured academic leader?

Sandra: My experience of him was that every year he challenged us. Every year, there was a new perspective or a consolidation or there was something else to do. There was never a time when I felt, well, now is the time to sort of just ease along.

He was watching her closely too, and saw her potential. She was a quick study, always had been, right back to her earliest days working with governments as a Price Waterhouse consultant where her duties had expanded fairly quickly. This pattern was repeated when she found herself back in the university sector in her early thirties. Within a short time Sandra was asked to be a course coordinator, and then acting head of department for six months at the age of thirty-two when the dean went overseas. Then, after a stint with her family in the US and Oxford, she returned to academia, convinced research was to be her metier. Again, her progress was very fast: she was asked to act as head of the School of Management and, again, she said yes. She found she enjoyed management, while so many of her academic colleagues would rather 'chew their arms off', as she puts it, than even think about it. Then the vital opportunity arrived, when the dean of business position came up. She got the job, and it led directly to deputy vice-chancellor. The rest is history. And the man who believed in her had a major role in the script.

Sandra: I don't to this day really know quite why but he did—it was such a funny thing. On his last overseas trip, I was with him at a graduation. He probably won't remember any of this. It was so meaningful for me though. I was in a taxi with him—we were going from one place to another in Singapore or Kuala Lumpur—and it seemed to me that he went out of his way to explain to me why he did things and why he didn't do things. He was just about to retire; it was like a summary.

Geraldine: Lucky you.

Sandra: It was a treasure chest for me, and when I first became dean I was standing next to him, coincidentally, getting a cup of tea—he was a very stoic person, a man of very few words—and he just said, well Sandra, when you're in management you're guilty. That's all he said, and I've lived off that for years.

It wasn't all sweetness and light between them, but a genuine working relationship; one full of typical struggles for power over territory and resources rather than one of master and protégée. This probably made it all the better as a preparation ground. Politics within universities is played pretty hard. They're baroque organisational beasts at many levels, akin to royal courts with elaborate structures. And they sport wins and losses that really matter to your status.

Sandra: So yes, as a dean I had a couple of fights—well, that's not my language, you know. I had a couple of moments with people, shall we say, one where I knew something was going to be taken out of my bailiwick and the responsibility handed over to somebody else. And I didn't think that was a sound decision. I still don't think it was the right decision. I lost that one, but I don't ever play the person, I play the position, and my feeling was at the time that the other person was playing the person. Some of this industrial relations stuff can get like that too. Another one, I won actually, was with the mentor who I am talking about. He wanted something to happen in the faculty and I disagreed. I told him that I disagreed and I told him why. He still didn't think my alternative was the right thing to do, and he could have pulled rank on me. But he didn't and, again, I learned something from him about negotiating.

Geraldine: He didn't pull rank?

Sandra: No, he did not. And when he left I remember him saying to me, you know you were right on that. And I was. I knew I was right. And so again, I say this when I talk to people about leadership: it's a very powerful thing when a leader can say, I was wrong, or a leader can say, I think your idea is the better one, or was the better one.

Fairness about gender at universities is very much a work-in-progress, in Sandra's view. She has no illusions about the path still to be travelled for women in academia, though she senses that some advances have been made in academic management roles. Before she arrived at JCU, one woman sat on the senior executive team. Sandra made it two when she became vice-chancellor, and now, she is pleased to say, women make up half the team. Sandra believes it is easier for other women once some females make it into the top leadership positions, and she is happy to mentor young women—and men—explaining her principles of leadership in the same way that she was bequeathed the wisdom by a generous mentor.

Sandra Harding emanates effortless authority, without an overt gravitas. Hers is a style based on competence and a sense that she won't be overwhelmed by the course of events. She projects an inherent sense of security within her demeanour, maybe the result of being a deeply loved person from a young age. One of her final remarks was revealing: 'Maybe this is a grave weakness of mine, but I don't take things personally, even when I should. I just can't afford to. If you were bowed by every sort of sling or arrow—I am actually quite good at objectifying things. But, this could be, in fact, a fatal flaw rather than a benefit.' This I doubt, though I also sense that she may not yet have been put to the fiery sword. So far, there may have been no dark night of the professional soul, the sort that tests abilities to the limit. It is hard to imagine her fully stretched like that. But in my personal experience and having watched others in authority, crises arrive when least anticipated and with terrible timing. They're generally unique in character, different from anything experienced previously. So rehearsing for them goes only so far. It may not come to that, ever, in Sandra's career. And knowing her, she won't be daunted, even in the face of temporary defeat. Her life seems well balanced; her courtesy a durable and invaluable quality as a leader and a woman.

CHAPTER 10

JULIE BISHOP

Compete and Thrive

Julie Bishop is currently Australia's foreign minister. Her political career began in 1998 when she was elected Liberal member for the seat of Curtin, in Western Australia. However, her first career choice was law, and she started out as solicitor at Adelaide firm Mangan, Ey and Bishop, where she became a partner. She moved to Perth where she was elected managing partner of Robinson Cox and served on various public entities, including the Senate of Murdoch University and as director of the SBS, before deciding that politics was where she could best serve the public.

THE spectacle of two women from opposite ends of the political spectrum simultaneously tilting at power and at each other is still rare theatre in Australia. The Julie Bishop versus Julia Gillard show turned out to be relatively short-lived. But while it lasted, it prompted some memorable commentaries, including those from women. Here's one of them, from the veteran Canberra insider Michelle Grattan, following an incident in parliament during the Rudd government in December 2008 that tapped into deep-seated stereotypes about female competitiveness: 'When Julie Bishop made a cat's claw gesture at Julia Gillard in Parliament this week, the shadow treasurer was giving one insight into why she's struggling politically. Bishop explained subsequently: "It is just a little thing that I do…suggesting that perhaps the girls should put the claws away." It sounded twee. I was reminded of the comment made by a well-placed observer recently when I was writing about Julia and Julie. "Gillard can mix it with the boys. Bishop can't. Gillard can cope in a man's world. Bishop is operating in a man's world."'[9]

Julia Gillard is now out of politics and ensconced in the more genteel business of memoir-writing and academia. Julie Bishop is certainly no longer struggling politically. She is bang in the middle of the ultimate male venue, international affairs, as our first female foreign minister. These two famous Adelaide women may seem to have come from different worlds, but they share an uncanny number of similarities. They are both lawyers, both buttressed by strong families, both very attractive to men, both childless and both described as 'deliberately barren' by a well-known Liberal senator. Julie Bishop tells me she called him following his remarks and admonished him. To the best of her knowledge, he never used the words again—either of her or the then prime minister.

Yet Julie Bishop and Julia Gillard represent very different ends of the South Australian capital's society. One springs from a small migrant family of considerable pride and potential, proving itself in a new land a long way from its native Wales: determined, canny, gritty, ready for combat. The other is steeped in the Adelaide Hills, four generations living within spitting distance of each other in the town of Basket Range. Orchardists and community activists, not quite Adelaide Establishment, they are proud of their heritage and ready to offer public service. The Bishops survived and rebuilt after the 1955 Black Saturday bushfires that razed their homes.

These women are not fans of each other, which was pretty clear from their televised parliamentary encounters, but there is some residual mutual respect, it would seem, merely for turning up to this male-dominated arena. I wonder: does class play a role here, or envy, of a very Adelaidian stripe? I always had the sense that Julia thought Julie was play-acting in her role on the opposite side of the chamber. Maybe many other Australians did too, though it would seem less so now with her ownership of the foreign affairs patch.

It would be a considerable mistake to underestimate the Member for Curtin and her years-long acquisition of leadership skills and aspirations, her seriousness and her exceptional competitiveness. She is a pretty quick study, like many lawyers, trained to grasp the essence of a brief fast. Julie Bishop has survived and thrived, though not without hiccups, due to a robust internal narrative of self-esteem. She believes in her bones that she has a right to be where she is and that she can contribute usefully: a core value derived straight from her family and bolstered by her legal training. There are marked similarities between some of her characteristics and those of the man who was her nemesis in the Liberal party for a while, John Howard. Like him, she actively looks forward to the next challenge, without over-thinking what got her into any past trouble. 'I don't do regrets', she's known to say. One of John Howard's political strengths was, supposedly, that he never made the same mistake twice, while simultaneously not ruminating over those mistakes.

During this term of government, how much will Julie apply these lessons to herself? Will she seek to bring new agendas to our foreign policy, which could be a risky strategy? How much will she be governed, as John Howard was, by an unerring instinct for knowing middle Australia's worries? In answer to the *Australian*'s Asian affairs analyst Rowan Callick's questioning of her underlying philosophy, she described her and her family's political credo as 'classic Menzies Liberals. We were steeped in small government, in lower taxes—I don't believe government should be at the heart of the economy, as Kevin Rudd said, or at the heart of society. I think it's a facilitator, and of course, a safety net. That's where we differ so strongly with our Labor counterparts who see it as an answer to all ills.'

Julie Bishop is a charming woman and this quality has served her well, say observers such as colleague Malcolm Turnbull, in building relationships with Australia's Pacific and Asian neighbours. She was determined to carve out a decent forty or so minutes from her schedule for me on the first day of the last session of Parliament for 2013, that exhausting year of politics. As I waited my turn, group after group was ushered in and out of her office, snatching rare time with her while she was in the country. Amid a sea of blandness, and even shabbiness, among the public servants and lobbyists, Julie is impeccably presented. It is hard not to notice and register the Everest-height black patent-leather shoes, her simple black skirt and beautifully tailored white-and-black tunic top. She is quintessentially well groomed and super fit; though her hair, which she has allegedly learned to blow dry efficiently each day, seems to attract disproportionate attention. Her image is of a predictable glamour that she can reliably reproduce, day in, day out. It suggests quite a bit about her choices and discipline. It also tells of a woman who has learned to limit any ragged edges that could be used against her.

The week we met, storms were erupting all around her. As foreign minister, she was at the centre of the Indonesia spying controversy that blew up in the wake of whistle-blower Edward Snowden's revelations. Escalating asylum-seeker crises were further testing Australia's relationship with its near neighbour; and the week before, there had been her well-publicised statements in Washington vigorously outlining why the United

States is our 'very best friend in the world' followed closely by Japan with no real mention of China: an omission laden with implied comment.

Appearances are important in this portfolio. It is a study in gravitas arguably on a par with the role of prime minister and even more so than that of the federal treasurer. The foreign minister has to encapsulate the dignity of the nation she/he represents. Demeanour genuinely matters in terms of perceived clout, and this equates directly to the ability to influence a course of events, which may involve matters of life and death. Former Labor foreign minister Bill Hayden once said that in foreign affairs 'words are like bullets'. More than in most other realms, your manner as chief diplomat—your perceived self-confidence and conviction about your country's right to influence—is critical. It is invariably a highwire act, a daunting but thrilling challenge, but one that in most cases is not conducted on your terms.

All these elements collided during a much-anticipated pre-election debate in August 2013 conducted by the Lowy Institute for International Affairs. The then Coalition shadow spokesperson Julie Bishop and the then foreign minister Bob Carr came together to canvass their different parties' takes on Australia's place in the world. As an observer, I found it quite gut-wrenching for reasons that took me by surprise. I, supposedly the dispassionate journalist, was incredibly nervous—on Julie's behalf! This was not my role. But female solidarity kicked in. For here she was, the first Australian woman in the running for this wonderful job, in the middle of what felt that night like an antipodean colosseum. And Julie was certainly not the typical gladiator; that role belonged to the super-experienced, ex–New

South Wales premier, Senator Bob Carr. He was in top form, exploiting his deep baritone voice to the full, tossing policy predictions, reflections and bon mots into the crowd of adoring acolytes, many of them younger men, who were dotted through the Victorian mansion's ground floor and first floor lounge. The odds were against the ALP in the election, but you'd never have known it from Carr's demeanour: every flourish, every statement, no matter on which sector of the world, was delivered with bravura.

The two combatants had been invited to present along typical debating lines, with timed primary statements on various issues followed by shorter rebuttals. It was both incredibly pressured and entertaining all at once. I wondered how Julie Bishop would counter this tour de force from Carr. There was really no trumping him, but she could not afford to be humiliated, and I don't think she was. She didn't 'win' as such, but neither did she lose, and she certainly portrayed herself as serious about the office that most likely awaited her after the election. With relief, I chalked it up as a good night for Australian women. And I learned quite a bit about Julie Bishop, primarily about her poise under pressure. In the intense atmosphere of the contest, she simply reverted to the notion of herself as advocate, sure of her talents and rights, under rules not dissimilar to those of a courtroom.

Julie Bishop's professional story started when she launched herself, young and purposeful, into the Adelaide Bar in 1979, having graduated with a bachelor of laws from the University of Adelaide. In this arena, her fighting spirit was forged. The traditional world she entered was not ready to give her its full respect. So she set out to prove her worth: a familiar refrain throughout her life.

Julie: The law firm that I worked in had been around for, you know, a hundred years. And I was the first female to be employed by that firm in any capacity other than as a typist or a cleaner. They'd never had a female clerk; they'd never had a female lawyer. I was the first. That was 1979.

Geraldine: Wow. What did you have to prevail over?

Julie: Senior male lawyers.

Geraldine: That was a quick reply.

Julie: One day, I was having some drinks with the lawyers and one of the very senior partners was lamenting the fact that a woman had been seen in the Adelaide Club. I was nonplussed, I was waiting for the 'and'. But he was just saying to the others, can you believe it, there was a woman at lunchtime in the Adelaide Club? I was waiting for everybody to say, and the point of this conversation is? But it didn't come. I wasn't naïve by any means, but I was still surprised that these attitudes prevailed. I tell this next story all the time. On my first night as an articled clerk, I went down into the boardroom with Andrew, another clerk. He was invited into a circle of lawyers, who were drinking whisky. He was invited into a circle—I was asked to serve the drinks.

It happened, and the fact that I'm still talking about it almost forty years later means I was just—mmm…

Still incandescent with rage, I would say, in a restrained Adelaide Hills way!

Geraldine: So you developed an armoury against that?

Julie: I just set out to prove them wrong—without being

aggressive or offensive or taking umbrage at it. I set out to show that their attitudes needed to be updated, to be a little more contemporary to reflect the reality of what was going on around them.

Julie Bishop affirms the powerful impact of a female role model on a younger woman's rise. Dame Roma Mitchell, that formidable legal contributor, deeply influenced her sense of what was possible, even if the younger woman didn't realise it at the time. I met Dame Roma just once, at a small farewell dinner for her in Sydney when she was stepping down as governor of South Australia. I recall a modest woman, anything but glamorous, but with a steadiness and a resolve that would have been very hard to rattle temperamentally, an ideal fit for the girl from Basket Range.

Julie: She was a towering figure, a towering intellect on the South Australian Supreme Court, the first woman to do so many things in South Australia. She was such an influence on me. I remember meeting her at a law society function, and she said that women can do anything that they set their mind to, that in the legal profession there are no barriers—there's no magic to it, you work hard, you put in the effort, you play to your strengths. All that sort of wonderful positive advice. I think she was the first female QC in Australia, certainly the first female Supreme Court judge in Australia. She was the first female chancellor of a university and first female governor, I think. I was always struck, going down into Supreme Court No 1 when Dame Roma was on the bench. She was formidable. Oh, absolutely. Didn't matter who she had sitting either side of her or if she was on the full court or how experienced the barrister was before her, she held her own and more. I admired her.

Despite this clear inspiration, Julie often felt very exposed, with so few women around her in the legal world. Her ballast, which fortified her so well for various assaults, was the certainty of her family's love. Her late mother, Isobel, her sisters and her brother have been her trusted sounding boards throughout her career. But the family influence runs much deeper than that. Community service is in her genes. Her grandfather was a dominant figure in the district and mayor of the local council for about thirty years. He'd even been a key supporter of long-term premier Sir Thomas Playford's entry into politics. He was on 'every committee you could think of: bushfire councils, apple-and-pear growers things. My father did a lot of that industry-body work too.' Civic commitment, dedicating your efforts to the betterment of your community, was valued above virtually all else, something Julie emphasised in her maiden speech in parliament.

But the big relationship was with her mother, Isobel, to whom she was exceptionally close. Isobel had suffered ongoing frustration in her own life and was determined that her daughter would not experience the same fate. Her drive towards achievement underpinned the household and especially young Julie. And Julie repaid her dues in what is an incredibly moving tale of reciprocal care, of daughter rescuing mother.

Julie: She was not able to achieve what she wanted to achieve. She was the youngest in quite a large rural family, in the mid north of South Australia. When she was sixteen or seventeen, her mother became very ill, and Isobel was called home. She had won a scholarship to Adelaide Girls High, a select high school in Adelaide, so she was obviously very bright. She did her Leaving and Leaving Honours at Adelaide Girls High and watched her best friends go on to university.

Her brothers were away at the war, one of her sisters was teaching, the other was married, so, instead of going to university, she stayed home and cared for her mother for a long time. I think it was very lonely for her, and she was also very disappointed and frustrated that she was not able to fulfil her ambitions. One of her girlfriends invited her to come down to Adelaide at some point, and that's when she met my father who'd just come back from the war. She was about twenty. She married at twenty-one. He was older, probably twenty-six or twenty-seven. And everything just went on as if there'd been no war. They got married in 1950 or thereabouts, and then my mother had four children, and she stayed home on the property. My father came from a longstanding agricultural-property family. We'd been there since the 1870s, and my mother's life for many years revolved around my father, the children and the property. It wasn't until I was about seventeen and at university—my sisters had gone off, my little brother was the last one at school—that my mother and I became quite close because I was the only one at home.

She told me how frustrated and disappointed she'd been in not getting a job and not being fulfilled and that's why she pushed us so hard to achieve, to do as well as we could. She was so keen for me to get into law school, because that's what she'd wanted to do. Her best friend at school, Ira Stephens, became a lawyer and a judge in South Australia. I'll never forget the day when we were sitting at home and she was going on—she was not complaining but it was sort of a lament that she'd never achieved—saying, you girls don't know how lucky you are and what opportunities you've got. And she said, I'll never be able to get a job, I'll never know whether I could have made it in the job world. I said, all right I've had enough of this. I got out the *Advertiser*, flicked through the paper and I said, I'm going to find you a job. And this is the weird thing: I found her a job! In the Situations Vacant there was a job for a mother figure—can you believe it—to run an after-school youth program for children in the Norwood area.

It was quite a progressive program at the time, and I said to my mother, yeah, go and apply for that job. Well, through my coaxing, and not telling my father, she applied for the job and she got it. And she spent about the next twenty years working her way up the Department of Community Welfare chain as a youth worker. She got involved in local politics; she became the local mayor. From the age of forty to fifty and onwards, she had the most fulfilling life.

So, with that story of achievement-against-the-odds in mind, in 1983, the good daughter moved to Western Australia, where she instantly experienced a more welcoming attitude towards female lawyers. She got a job immediately, after redoing her Articles under different regulations in Western Australia. One of Perth's biggest firms, Robinson Cox, became her employer, and, after eighteen months, she was made a partner. Meanwhile, the numbers of women studying law was increasing dramatically. Women, Julie estimates, made up more than fifty per cent of graduates in law schools across the country, and she sensed that the gender balance was moving significantly in the right direction.

Julie married property developer Neil Gillion, though that union was to break up and she never married again. Whatever she feels privately, she does not betray any grief over this facet of her life. She has no regrets, though she did admit to me that self-doubt could definitely accompany her. But self-pity was simply not admitted. She'd made choices and sacrifices; she'd gone down paths that had excluded her from other paths, possibly children. 'But at the end of the day, they are decisions that I have taken, and I do believe you are in charge to a certain extent of your own destiny.'

Western Australia turned out to be Julie's land of opportunity. As the century was drawing to a close, Robinson Cox's culture gave her permission to strive. Nothing was deemed out of bounds. And she consciously fostered a pattern of aspiring to positions that people might have thought beyond her, like managing partner. The same grit that withstood the conservative men of Adelaide law resurfaced. After all, she exclaimed, why would she put herself in a position if there was a strong possibility of failure?

Julie: I believe I'd proven myself through a number of cases and my client list and workload. I believe that I was up there with the best of them. So when I became a partner—I think five of us became partners at the same time, three guys and two women—there was no question that I felt very confident I'd been appointed for all the right reasons. Likewise, when I became the managing partner in 1994, there was an election within the firm. Two male partners stood, and I had to run a campaign. It was my first, and they played hard. There was no quarter given because I would have been the first female in that position. And that was fine. When I was elected, I felt very comfortable that I'd done it on the criteria that my partners would be looking for in any managing partner.

One level of confidence led to another—and to another challenge. Julie was asked to chair the Town Planning Appeal Tribunal, a quasi-judicial position, and her appointment ruffled feathers.

Julie: I was a solicitor in a law firm, and the deputy of the tribunal at the time was a very learned academic, steeped in years of experience in town planning. When I was appointed as chair he was rightly miffed and raised it with me.

Geraldine: He said, what do you think you're doing?

Julie: Yeah, exactly. He thought he should have been appointed chair, and who did I think I was, and what's my background, what's my experience? And I said, I'm being asked to chair a board that hears applications, takes evidence and makes a decision and writes judgments, and I believe I've got the relevant experience to do it. He couldn't believe it. He said, you can't possibly be going into this field so naively. But I didn't see it that way. I wouldn't have done it if I didn't think I had the capacity to do it. I size up situations and opportunities and say to myself, do you think you have the capacity to do that? And if I'm confident that I do, I'll do it. I didn't see it

> as me having to be an expert on town planning per se. It was always a three-person tribunal. I had expert help available. Mine was a chair's role, which was to conduct the hearings. I'd been a litigator all my career, so I knew how to conduct hearings, to take and assess evidence and weigh up competing arguments and the like. And so that was the way I saw the role, which was different from the way he saw the role. It's just an interesting conversation. Now, he's a very dear friend of mine. We came from opposite ends of the political spectrum, but we ended up firm friends.

Then she turned forty and, despite the overt success, the connections, the good life of Perth, something changed. Who really knows why turning points occur when they do? But for Julie Bishop, this significant birthday ushered in a time of restlessness. Some impulse would not be suppressed, even if she couldn't quite identify what it was. And a solution to her ennui was defying her. Right back to her early school days, she'd taken charge in her circle (president of the debating team, captain of netball, the organiser of the year-twelve singing and dancing review, the teacher of scripture at age ten). She sensed some leap into the unknown was now called for.

She turned for help to two West Australian business stalwarts: Denis Horgan, from Leeuwin Estate winery, and Michael Chaney, chancellor of the University of Western Australia, ex-head of Wesfarmers and now chair of the NAB. They each suggested she consider one of the advanced business courses at Harvard or Stanford or INSEAD, the elite French business school. Chaney told her about his Harvard experience, which had been life changing. In fact, he warned her that if she went she may well not return to her original career. And that is exactly what happened. The executive education course at Harvard consistently invited her to consider how her skills could better society, not merely herself. And at the end of it, it wasn't the corporate world that beckoned, as she'd imagined.

> Julie: So I went off to Harvard, and it was a fantastic experience because, after all these years of intensive legal practice, I was on my own. You weren't meant to contact your office, so I had to leave all that behind—family, friends, everything—and spend three months, at the age of forty, being a student. It was highly competitive. It was a fascinating time, and it was there that I decided no, it's not corporate that I want to do—it's back to community service and public office.

Thus, Julie Bishop became the Liberal member for Curtin within two years of completing her Harvard course, after much discussion with her family and after overturning the sitting member, Alan Rocher, a loyal friend of John Howard's. It was a messy time for West Australian Liberals, and Julie wasn't exactly seen as a prize selection. But she was up for it all, another example of her steely conviction about her rightful place in the world. While she is the ultimate networker—'she pretty much knows everybody,' says Perth heavy-hitter John Poynton—she picks and chooses her real intimates. 'With Julie,' a close friend told Fairfax journalist Deborah Snow, 'there is a level to which you get let in and then there is the level below that she does not share. It's all part of her discipline. She doesn't let her guard down.'

That probably fortifies her well against what simply goes with the territory of modern political stardom: the criticisms that accompany a cabinet post. Sometimes a psychoanalytical tone creeps into the searching personal profiles of modern politicians, which can be searing. This may apply to both women and men. But when women are the targets, the details can become so precise as to make me wince. Here's what a senior Labor woman told Deborah Snow: 'There's still a lot of the head girl about her. I think she's worked out that to be successful in the Liberal Party you can only be a particular type of woman and she's going to be the best example of that she can possibly be. It's about flirting a little bit, about personal presentation, about willingness to attack Labor. It's this perfectionist approval-seeking kind of persona with a very particular desire for approval from men.' I admit that I would prefer not to read that if it was about me; I have read some fairly character-building verdicts on my media career, but none quite like that.

Julie: I'd read something like that and thought, well, they don't know me. That's obviously written by somebody who wants to portray me in a particular light. If you knew me, I don't think you'd say that about me. Certainly, my friends and colleagues wouldn't say that. It's an easy criticism to make. The head prefect—well, I was a head prefect at a girls' school so they're stereotyping me in that regard. But as for this seeking approval, think of the women who've made it to the top in the Liberal Party. I don't think that you could see a common theme that we succumb to that type of behaviour.

Geraldine: And, of course, some of your friends do say that the woman they know is not that hard-faced person people see on television, because they know, in fact, a carefree person, who loves a party and being sociable.

Julie: Yeah, well, I have a very serious job. I'm the deputy leader of a major political party that is now in government. I have been a cabinet minister; now I'm the minister for foreign affairs. These are serious, weighty, portfolios and there's no room for frivolity. So, yes, I'm on television in my role as a minister of the Crown and I take that very seriously. If I were frivolous on television, could you imagine the criticisms I would garner?

Geraldine: But men are allowed to be frivolous aren't they?

Julie: Do you really want to be called a bimbo every time you open your mouth? I do have a very serious job and I take it very seriously. I don't take anything for granted in terms of the privilege that I've been afforded by being a cabinet minister in government.

And there's more, as the saying goes: more free character analysis from her own side, let alone her enemies, a point made by the journalist Annabelle Crabb in September 2013: 'Julie Bishop is a woman who has never, as far as I can recall, had a concession made to her on account of her gender. In fact I cannot even recall any instances of chivalry towards her displayed by her male colleagues, many of whom have cheerfully undermined and white-anted her just as viciously as they would any man whose job they wanted.' There is a terrible analogy used about her: that she's a cockroach; that she'll shed skins and survive anything. I put this to her and it prompted a fascinating exchange.

Julie: I know exactly where it came from.

Geraldine: I detect you'll get back at them?

Julie: In more ways than they'll ever know. I'm a don't-get-mad-get-even type.

Geraldine: So, you do remember these insults? And you bide your time?

Julie: Oh, yes. There are times when you just have to keep things to yourself, and I certainly don't let on that things disturb me or upset me. This is a very competitive environment, one of the most competitive I've ever come across. So you've got to be able to maintain your equilibrium and not get consumed by petty comments that people make. You have to really believe in yourself and trust your judgment and your own instincts and I do that. So when comments like that are made, you put yourself in the shoes of the person making them and you understand where they're coming from, and it just gives you strength to deal with it.

The stakes can be exceptionally high. After all, she has been deputy to three very different leaders: Brendan Nelson, Malcolm Turnbull and Tony Abbott. The dramatic 2009 leadership battle, which Turnbull lost by one vote to Abbott, was followed by a similarly emotional denouement, because Turnbull was convinced that Julie had ratted and voted against him. Julie insisted that the voting slips be retrieved and put on display, to prove to him that she'd stayed true.

Julie: The election of the deputy is a separate election. I didn't run on a ticket with Brendan, I didn't run on a ticket with Malcolm and I didn't run on a ticket with Tony. My election as deputy was separate, so I pitched myself to the backbenchers, saying, whoever is the leader of the party you need stability in the deputy's role and I can offer that. I knew that we would go through tumultuous times, because Brendan won by a vote, Malcolm lost by a vote. But if you're looking for stability and a rock, then I can offer that.

Geraldine: So you worked out your pitch.

Julie: Absolutely—and it was also the feedback I got from colleagues about where they saw me. In 2007 there were colleagues asking me to run for leader. I took soundings from all my colleagues; they knew that there were going to be battles at the leadership level and they wanted me to be deputy, to be the ballast if you like, for the storms ahead. And, well, I guess it speaks for itself. I'm still there.

Indeed she is. But does she 'recognise herself', that terrific Julia Gillard summary of her personal bottom line? 'Yes, I'm still the little girl from Basket Range, with hopes, dreams, aspirations. I haven't lost touch with who I am and my upbringing and the values I've had all my life. I can recognise myself without doubt.' Her family apparently expected this pretty, enthusiastic daughter to marry and have kids as a matter of course. That didn't happen. I wonder whether they fully recognised how crucial her arrival at the Adelaide Bar would prove to be in triggering in their adored daughter and sister her tribal nature and her competitiveness—qualities that mean she should never, ever be underestimated.

CHAPTER 11

HILDA SCOTT

Authority of a Different Kind

Sr Hilda Scott is a professed sister with the enclosed Benedictine Order of nuns, based at Jamberoo, south of Sydney. However, this position followed several other career experiences, including an early but abandoned start as a nun with the Sisters of Mercy at the age of nineteen. Having decided it wasn't for her, she turned to youth work with street kids, then kindergarten teaching and more formal social work, before deciding her vocation lay with an enclosed order. She joined the Benedictines in 1991.

OBEDIENCE to higher authorities did not feature within my research as key advice for modern leaders. Nor did notions of humility. Or abandonment. Hardly surprising. They don't fit the spirit of our times. 'I did it my way', the line from Sinatra's signature hymn of the mid twentieth century, captures much better the Western zeitgeist. Independently choosing your own path is now feted as delivering liberation and creativity to you and your community. Individual sovereignty is enshrined in laws and presented as a core, underlying principle in modern societies. Even though the latest work on leadership emphasises the idea of leader-as-servant, as facilitator of others' talents, leaders are presumed to be those who can grab the initiative. They are expected to set a roadmap for those around them, with close assistance from respected collaborators.

However, other models of leadership have remained faithful to very different guiding principles, passed down from the great monasteries of medieval Europe. The enclosed order of

Benedictine nuns of Jamberoo Abbey, one hundred kilometres south of Sydney, is an example of one such model. Its inhabitants operate under the venerable Rule of St Benedict, devised in the turbulent sixth century when the collapse of the Roman Empire had brought chaos.

One afternoon, last summer, in the convent's reception room, over delicious brewed tea and homemade muffins, kindergarten-teacher-turned-enclosed-nun Sr Hilda Scott outlined why Benedict's Rule, one of the most famous documents of the Christian world, provides a roadmap for life and leadership. She believes it offers wisdom for all ages and talents, though she doesn't really care whether other people see it like that or not. As one of the community's leaders, her serenity does not rest on the secular world's usual definitions of success: have I been effective today; have I advanced my talents; where did the day 'move' me on my journey towards self-fulfilment; have I impressed others? She is free of all that, yet utterly committed to her calling. That's the yield of consciously including obedience, humility, abandonment to a transcendent power, the dignity of work and routine, and, above all, God in her life.

Hilda: The truth for me is that I don't want to be a leader, Geraldine. I just want to be a good monk. I just want to be somebody who, when her number's up, can look God dead in the eye and say, I love you. I want to know that through me He has brought about in the lives of other people whatever it is that He wants to bring about. If He so chose to put leadership into my life He'd know what He was doing, but I don't want to be a leader. I just want to be a good monk, and that's not garbage-bag humility. That's a fact.

This philosophy means that Hilda and her colleagues operate in a very different system from that of the world outside when taking on responsibility for others. And it is a challenging model for any modern Australian woman to abide by. I feel sure that I could not live by it, with its 4 am reflection to start the day, as well as five other prayer rituals dotted through the day, and all the discipline. Still, it prompts reflection on the meaning of striving and ambition and the nobility or otherwise of aspiring to lead at all.

In the convent, when an abbess dies a solemn process is triggered. No one puts up their hand and says, I'm ready for leadership. That judgment lies in the whole community's hands, through an election. The nuns nominate, via secret ballots, who should lead them in the future. There is no lobbying and every fully professed woman under the age of seventy-five is eligible to be nominated. When the long-serving Mother Benedicta died in 2006, a remarkably introspective process was set in motion.

Hilda: What we do is we look inside ourselves to ask, how am I living a monastic life? It's an opportunity for me, for each one of us, to reaffirm our living of a monastic life. When we've done that, then we go in and we elect an abbess, but we do it from a place of utter freedom. We're not going in there to push a favourite or anything. In having come to look at how we live a monastic life we get a sense of what we'd like to see in our overall living of monastic life.

Geraldine: So you're identifying with the broader entity rather than just the individual?

Hilda: Yes, that's right.

Last time, it took two ballots before Mother Mary Barnes was elected. I approached Sr Mary for this interview. She declined but was happy for Sr Hilda to be the focus. Hilda's face is the one often associated with the enclosed abbey, due to her online blogs and her appearances in the 2007 ABC-TV Compass series *The Abbey*, over which she was effectively put in charge. The series aired over five Sundays to strong ratings. It was a real pleasure to introduce it each week. It followed five typical Australian women seeking spiritual retreat and refreshment over several weeks at Jamberoo Abbey, bringing the television audience into a monastery's rhythms. It was similar in format to a BBC documentary at Jamberoo's brother monastery in Worth, in southern England, with five British men and a charismatic abbot, Dom Christopher Jamison. Ironically, maybe because of the huge publicity afforded the Worth Benedictine abbey and its principles, its monk community deposed Christopher Jamison as abbot shortly after the series aired. Even though he was a model of discretion, Fr Jamison was clearly quite shattered, as were many others looking on. No one has ever really explained what happened, but, on that occasion, the group certainly trumped the individual, and pretty savagely.

Hilda: Christopher was the abbot for the time. There was a great deal that needed to be done within his community and he did it. Now, with every leader there comes a time when you've done what you were there to do and then the monks say, thank you, now we need the baton to be handed on to someone who will take us down another road. We're going to build on what you've done, but if we hang on to you, we won't go down the road we now know we're being called to.

Like abbots, abbesses have real power within their communities. Each one carries a staff, a symbol from the days when abbesses had the authority of bishops. In European monasteries, some abbesses even wore mitres and had temporal as well as spiritual power in those pre-Enlightenment days.

Hilda: My own namesake, Saint Hilda, was a force to be reckoned with. She ran the whole town of Whitby, in northern England, including a double monastery of men and women. There were monks under her, and priests.

Geraldine: What era are we talking about?

Sr Hilda: We're talking the 600s AD. Double monasteries were out, I would say, by the years 900 to 1000, as women, of course, lost their status. The men were coming back from the crusades and so women's status was going down. But in the early days they had real power. The other thing, of course, is that the staff is a symbol of shepherding.

Geraldine: And it symbolises an absolute authority, I suppose?

Sr Hilda: Yes, we're not a democracy, and, yes, it does. There are big decisions, and a wise leader takes those decisions, in consultation with other people.

Geraldine: So would you say it's collegiality rather than a democratic spirit at work?

Hilda: Yes, I would. In a monastery, if democracy is emphasised, we lose the life.

Geraldine: I don't claim to understand that, but I will accept your word for it.

Hilda: I mean that you can't have everybody just going off and doing precisely what they want to do.

Geraldine: So obedience is pretty important?

Hilda: Oh, yes, yes, very important. Remember that the Latin word *obsculta* guides us in our Rule. It means both obedience and listening. We don't do things because the abbess tells us; we do them because we consider hers to be the voice of God. So if she's telling us, we're listening. She, likewise, has a responsibility to listen to us and to listen to God.

Geraldine: There's no arguing with her—ultimately, she has the last word, hasn't she?

Sr Hilda: She's got the last word. Yes.

Yes, the absolute authority of the monastery is a very different model from that of the wider world, and thank goodness for that, by and large. I give three cheers to have been born post-Enlightenment, with the power of the Church and aristocracy checked and with the prioritising of rational thought and the rights of individual conscience: I can't really imagine life without these rights. But for all her commitment to the Benedictine Rule, Sr Hilda respects the secular world and feels pretty connected to it. She is no hermit. Her duties hinge on 'formation', as she describes her work both with people wanting to join her community and with those who seek its counsel from outside. That work places her 'slap bang right into the middle of humanity'.

Over the course of any year, hundreds of people bring their troubles to the nuns. They stay in cottages on the Jamberoo Abbey estate, observing silence, worshipping alongside the nuns, and being counselled. This enclosed Benedictine community constantly serves, but without any marketing of themselves or evangelising.

Sr Hilda has a good line on her blog about ultimately choosing a real life instead of a safe one. 'You can run for so long,' she wrote recently, 'but you have to stop for a moment of truth at some stage, asking yourself, do I want a life or don't I?' She speaks from experience, having decided about twenty years ago that her journey from Sydney-based bank clerk to social worker dealing with kids on the streets, to kindergarten teacher, then to the Parramatta Sisters of Mercy, should take her to the enclosed Benedictines. It was a momentous commitment and she has never regretted it. It gives her an ideal balance between personal growth and service to others.

Hilda: Well, there's a misconception about what it actually means to be a good governor of others, a good leader. Ironically, I've yet to come across a workable definition that satisfies me. I think that to be a good leader you have to be somebody who has gone through the seasons. You also have to be somebody who is prepared to still go through the seasons, not somebody who says, I have arrived, therefore the rest of you will arrive by the same road. That's not leadership. Leadership says, hey, you've come by different roads; this is what those roads have done to you; and I've got a sense of how that might be because this is what the road has done to me—come with me. Now, let's be open not only to the seasons ahead of us, but let's embrace together what the seasons will do to us. That implies a leadership that's here in the middle, not a leadership that's up there.

Geraldine: It's a sort of mutual journey that involves a genuine humility, together with a yielding to whatever might be asked of you.

Hilda: Yes.

Geraldine: And developing the habit of relinquishing control, in the nature of abandoning yourself to your god, which I think is quite a hard concept for modern people to grasp—how does that help?

Hilda: Maybe I could provide an analogy to illustrate what I mean. When I was learning to swim, one of the things I picked up was that when I got into trouble, I could fight and fight and fight and fight and fight to get myself out of trouble, and after a while I learnt that if I just lay back, relaxed and floated, then I came out safe every time. It's the same when you're going through the waves, you know, if you abandon yourself to the wave you won't get hurt. That's my imagery. My own life experience has taught me that I can rail against the things that happen to me, against the things that cause a broken heart, the things that turn my life upside down. I can try to make sense of it. I can do all of that, and that's got its value. But what has worked for me is to go to God and say, I believe utterly in your love for me, because I've made so many mistakes in life and I'm actually standing here intact—this is a miracle in itself, so I know you've stood by me, and I'm giving myself over to you.

Geraldine: So it is not despair?

Hilda: Oh, far from it. It is the exact opposite. It's hope—it's hope big-time. And, as Paul says, we are never deceived in our hope.

Of course, for many women, especially those growing up Catholic in my era, the concept of yielding to your fate, or floating with the metaphorical rip, tended to mean something different in reality from what Hilda describes. It usually translated to, give up your ambition, rather than go for it. Because stepping up just might introduce that dreaded vice, *vanity*. You might get 'above yourself', which was the ultimate no-no. It takes many years to pick apart the mixed messages bequeathed by such an education. Oddly enough, the nuns of my era were often quite subversive role models, whether or not they realised it. They could be severe and their authority was complete. But, at the same time, Catholic girls saw them as women governing their own realm, which they didn't see a lot of elsewhere in the community. The nuns were strong and decisive. I think their influence played a considerable role in the disproportionately high numbers of Catholic women who emerged as early public achievers, women such as Susan Ryan, Germaine Greer, Judy Davis, and former state premiers Carmen Lawrence and Clare Martin. The nuns embodied the idea that authority was worthwhile.

But it was a mixed message, which I couldn't help reflecting on as I re-entered a convent precinct like the abbey. In my memory, within girls' schools of all varieties, the dark arts of neither politics nor strategic thinking were considered useful concepts to grasp. Whereas, Protestant and Anglican men describe a tone of solemn challenge issued to them at school: when will *you* speak truth to power? How will you leave the world a better place? What is being asked of you, personally, to contribute? The big invitations of my school life were about giving back to others—of those to whom much is given, much will be asked—as well as the need to rise above everyday troubles.

Women in the Catholic tradition I grew up in, including Hilda, were notionally encouraged to reach for the stars in doing their duty, to never hold back. But that rarely included governing others outside their orders, and certainly not governing men. This observation was not lost on Hilda, neither was its legacy. It was the only time I saw her bristle about conditions inside the Church.

> Hilda: Let's face it, in times gone by, where did women have any real say? Sisters working in parishes could see the real story inside people, could see the real story within the parish. But really, who listened to them? Nobody much. They were powerless. They joined the powerlessness of the laypeople in the Church, and, to that extent, we were glad, because we don't want to be separated from the people. Society told us that the male way was the right way, and we bought into it. Thank God we're not buying into it any more.

She had one keen reflection that set me thinking. It relates to the impact of fathers versus mothers in forming a readiness for leadership, or, more precisely, the impression gleaned by the growing girl about where authority lay within her family and how she thought about her apprenticeship, as it were.

> Hilda: I've heard people say, what would my father do? It was not, what would my mother do? I mean, I've done it myself: gee I wonder what Dad would have said about this? Measuring myself against some standard, saying to myself, well, no, Dad wouldn't have had a bar of that, so neither will I.
>
> Geraldine: Even though often the mothers have possibly been very strong, particularly I think, in Irish–Catholic families.
>
> Hilda: Yes. Indeed.

What a puzzle this is. It explains why so many women have not rehearsed the lines and images of leadership, unlike so many men who have taken up office-bearing positions in their sporting clubs during adolescence and their twenties, and sampled power. I am sure these lines can be learned. But it probably means that women must continue the process of renovating femininity's imagery to fit better the likely challenges. Hilda had one last piece of advice: don't think you can or need to do it solo.

> Hilda: One of the great premises in the spiritual life is that nobody should walk the road on their own. There must always be an elder somewhere, somehow, with whom you're in touch. The role of that elder is to continually steer you. You go along and say, A, B, C and D. And the elder will say, well, actually what you're talking about is E, F, G and not A, B, C at all. If you're sincere and truly seeking that deeper relationship, you will listen. You will change accordingly. I think the clue is in the sincerity of your search.

For Hilda, the search is all about the transfiguring of the self, of understanding the difference between outright ambition, which may involve long-held dreams, and going beyond the 'me, me, me', as she puts it, to leadership through service. A kind of metamorphosis needs to occur in people who seek to lead—as seen in the symbolism of death and resurrection common to all the great religious traditions, as well as in the Greek myths of Thanatos and Eros. Risk is a necessary companion, and courage is required. Is it any wonder most of us choose not to travel that path?

CHAPTER 12

CHRISTINE JENKINS

Leading though Healing

Christine Jenkins AM is a senior staff specialist at Concord Hospital and professor of respiratory medicine at Sydney University's faculty of medicine. She was educated at Sydney's Hornsby Girls High School and went on to choose a challenging path, specialising in thoracic medicine. Christine has participated in or led many expert panels on asthma, obstructive lung disease, drug development, therapeutic guidelines for lung health, and translational research. She headed the profession's peak organisation, the Thoracic Society (2006–10), and is currently in charge of respiratory trials at Sydney's George Institute for Global Health.

HOW to establish the credibility required for leadership in the demanding world of modern science, while trying to live a balanced life? How to earn the respect of one's peers in medicine, the bedrock for building the legitimacy required for leadership? And how to do all this while simultaneously managing family, friendships and her own good health? Another challenge has been maintaining the faith that initially drove her, the Anglicanism of her outer Sydney childhood and adolescence. It has been a small casualty of her super busy life but what a powerful sense of duty it has left her with. All these questions and issues have preoccupied Dr Christine Jenkins throughout her glittering career as thoracic physician and researcher. And they still do.

Christine adores her work, without reservation. She believes it's worthwhile because it is people-centred and it helps the world to thrive. What a powerful cocktail to motivate a life-long commitment. She hasn't needed to wrestle much with a search for meaning within the medical profession: helping to improve people's lives is hard to beat for job satisfaction. But medicos work in a highly competitive arena. Their contribution and talents, and therefore their professional status, is constantly under the scrutiny of their colleagues. When these innate rivalries are combined with the altruism that marks medicine, we, the community, benefit from the resulting research advances.

But even though teamwork is emphasised far more these days than it was, say, a generation ago, this field is dominated by some very big egos. Many of them belong to the classic dominant men, the uber-tough male specialists, so often featured as characters in television series and movies. Doctors can seem like miracle workers—why wouldn't they develop some 'attitude'? But, at heart, they know they don't work magic; they know what they don't know. Specialists seek to advance the cause of science, and see no need to apologise for insisting on high professional standards and total commitment from their colleagues.

This is Christine's world. If you wish to rise through the ranks, as Christine has, it seems you cannot aspire to live a quiet life, focusing on your specialist skills. You have to join in the politics of the profession and the collegial structure with all its conferences, here and overseas. It is a recipe for a lifestyle that is particularly tough for mothers. Christine's average week includes public clinics, supervising medical students, writing research papers and monitoring doctoral theses, as well as various duties for the professional bodies she belongs to. It is a schedule that leaves me, a busy friend, exhausted. Often she is exhausted too, but she keeps going, with a 'whatever it takes' attitude.

During conference times, the pressure rises: Christine regularly gives at least four major addresses to the thousands of attendees at these events, as well as preparing up to four shorter descriptions of research projects. Throw in several meetings and it's no wonder she indulges in some serious hiking, in Yosemite or the Swiss Alps, to wind down when all is done.

So, why does a talented doctor with a glowing reputation accept these punishing and relentless schedules? What gains are on offer if you do establish your authority within this demanding realm? The yield is pretty seductive: first, there's the possibility of making real progress in community health; and second, there's a powerful sense of *virtue* in being the noble healer. But the question that fascinates me is how can women coming through the ranks of this world realistically aim for leadership positions while still participating meaningfully in family and community lives? What are the secrets of those who make it?

> Christine: I am driven by a strong sense of duty; whether it always has a religious base or needs to have one I'm less sure of, because I think duty can certainly be a highly valued civic quality and doesn't require a Judeo or Christian sort of understanding of the world. But I do think you need that dutiful ethic. I think a sense of civic duty is the ideal, in the Greek sense: that's what I'd want to advocate.
>
> Do I think men have less of that? No, I don't. What I think they are much better at is just the practicalities of things. So, for instance, when somebody asks me to take on an extra task—say, the small detail of putting a meeting into my diary—I will look at it and think, I could do that teleconference at 11 pm or I could do it at 5 am or I could write that paper after dinner or on my weekend. I'm not sure guys are thinking like that.

Geraldine: Why aren't they?

Christine: They might be. But I think they have just a more categorical sense of practical possibilities, and I think that serves them very well in many situations; it limits what they take on.

Geraldine: Is it that they don't think they have to prove themselves, don't need the approval that will come with taking on everything?

Christine: I don't know how much men who are very high achievers feel they are driven by a need or desire for approval. I think even I would say, I don't need or desire to be approved, but I certainly don't want to be disapproved of, and there's a difference. I am not likely to drive another person to change their plans. Without wanting to get too much into generalities about men and women and how differently they respond to tiny microcosm examples, I think men are more likely to say, no, I can't do 5 pm on a Friday night. Whereas a woman says, oh, well, that fits with 8 am in London so I suppose I could do that telecon then. Women are constantly thinking of consequences: why that might be a good time for everyone else and, therefore, wouldn't it be better just to fit in with that. Now whether men do that as well, I don't know.

What is common to both genders, Christine insists, and very important for legitimacy in the field of science, is a demonstrated proficiency in key skills within your particular discipline: skills that are explicit, practised and evaluated over and over again. Staff specialists and professors like Christine are accorded immense respect within medicine, proportionally more than might flow to, say, the veteran journalist or accountant. But it comes with strings attached. Christine must still conduct complex procedures on sick patients in front of her junior staff, must contribute to the big multidisciplinary meetings before all her peers, and has only just managed to remove herself (after thirty years) from the on-call monthly roster that ate into her weekends and holidays. The field of expertise shifts fast in medicine. And no quarter is given to people who appear to slip—in medicine, the injunction to actively attend to your skill base is no idle mantra. And if neglected, leadership is out of the question.

> Christine: In lung health, in science generally, I would say, there are a number of attributes that the really great leaders have. First of all, they have got to be highly, highly skilled in their core area of expertise, which happens to be being a scientist. That involves not just intellectual firepower, which they inevitably do have, but also the capacity to be successful in the grant application process through to implementing studies effectively, getting results, getting published, and having work that is seen to be a major contribution. To be a leader, it is really important that your peers and colleagues respect you. Now, perhaps, if you're not absolutely stand-out and at the forefront in a particular discipline, people will still respect you if you have other major attributes: if you can train young scientists, or build a program, if you have a laboratory or a team who really work well together and where you are supervising younger students—PhD students, post-doctoral students, masters students, even encouraging undergraduate students and giving them experience and inspiring them to stay in science.

So I would say the qualities for leadership are intellect, inspiration and, if I am going to stick with the 'i's, I would also need to say implementation—the capacity to actually make your science work. Ideally, I think leaders have another capacity: translational capacity. They need to actually talk about how this piece of work is going to slot into the overall understanding of something and result in a better outcome for the community, the world, or even some small group of people. It doesn't have to be 'the world'—that's a bit grandiose. But a real leader can actually see the follow-through, isn't just doing something obscure which is scientifically fascinating, but is actually thinking, how will this translate into something meaningful?

This is clearly a broad brief—daunting, to my mind. But it doesn't end there, in Christine's view. You cannot presume the extra respect of peers that would presage leadership, she says, without also operating beyond your specialist area.

Christine: I think it is harder to be a true leader if you are just an excellent clinician. You need to be an advocate as well, and to be able to articulate a certain ambition for the future. It doesn't have to be blue sky; it just needs to be another step forward to a point that is achievable, within reach, but perhaps not something everybody has been thinking about or believes can be moved towards. You have got to bring people along with you; that's an essential element towards leadership.

This is the area that the McKinsey Research Team's Women Matter 2 project noted could still be rather wanting in otherwise high-achieving women at times of work crisis or challenge: that capacity to stand out from the crowd and to 'envision' what might come next, whether or not it was in the original plan, and to do so in a way that brings people along with you.[10]

Christine: I'm not at all sure that is true in medicine and science. I can easily think of women I know, who are quite close to me, who have really taken people along with them. And I have seen people in health-care environments do the same thing. In health service delivery, especially, I think women get quite passionate about issues of quality of care and service delivery, and can often be very influential with administrations. They are willing to engage and to bash their head against the brick wall that health administration can really feel like at times.

Geraldine: And you think they grasp the need to bring people along? It's a seductive process: gathering people to reform or change or anything that is a break from the status quo.

Christine: Well, I think that is a big challenge, and I am not sure whether men would describe it that way. I personally find it a challenge. I think that inspiring people—having the gravitas, the respect, the momentum, and bringing all those things together to make them work for you in terms of affecting change among your colleagues and peers—is one of the biggest challenges of all, and I don't think of myself as very good at it. I would like to be a lot better at it, and I often muse on the intrinsic capabilities that are required.

It's not so much that leaders have to prove that they

are fantastic clinicians or surgeons to start with, but the drive that facilitates their becoming fantastic surgeons is the same drive that causes them to think, how can I make this work more effectively in the bigger picture?

Geraldine: Except that, as we are talking, I realise that often the visionary is not the process person, and the ideal is to have the two working side by side. But you're saying that both qualities have to be present in a leader?

Christine: Look, this might be one of the reasons why people who have never been trained in medicine and who are health administrators probably complain about doctors, and certainly doctors complain about them. But I have to say the culture is such that in general you are most likely to be able to take your colleagues and others in the vicinity along with you in medicine if you have earned respect in your basic skills area to start with. You don't have to be top of the pile, but if you pursue your clinical career, and gradually see the problems that need to be addressed, engage yourself and keep on being engaged, then people see you bringing off a few small wins over time. And those small gains turn into bigger opportunities. And you gradually acquire the sort of respect that means you get elected into various positions of leadership.

It sounds to me like a very masculine model. No doubt practitioners will say it has guaranteed high standards and that we are discussing core, universal competencies that are not restricted to one gender. But I wonder how many women it repels? Conscientious individuals can make a difference, but the overall system, Christine believes, is not geared to graciousness, or to allowing a balanced life. Or to offering praise to each other: simple acts of acknowledgement can be immensely affirming to young colleagues, and Christine tries to remember how much they mattered to her as she entered her medical career, four decades ago.

> Christine: I think we often reflect in medicine on the fact that we all work too hard, that we all take on too much. We have exceptionally high expectations of ourselves and we lose sight of the fact that we are probably at one end of the spectrum in relation to this. When we look within our professional community, we don't realise that we are at one extreme end. And we sometimes fail ourselves by not being able to get a balanced view of things and to say, this is ridiculous: I am working too hard; I am trying to do too much. In my mini-context of medicine, this doesn't look extreme but the fact is, it is. Now people in business might feel the same way too, I'm sure they do at the top of business.

Over the years, as Christine's status as a medical leader steadily increased, I watched the invitations flood into her always-overflowing inbox. She is asked to participate in and lead a bewildering array of ventures: international drug overview committees, seminars to educate local GPs on the latest asthma research, federal government committees evaluating Australia's readiness for the next pandemic. The events in question take place in school holidays, on weekends and at nights, complicating her routinely over-full schedule and challenging her family life. For quite a few years, almost all of this extra work was performed pro bono. This is admirable, at some levels, and necessary where conflicts of interests with drug company sponsorship is a real issue. But Christine's good nature was exploited, in my view. And it took a long time for her to believe she could fairly ask for monetary recompense for lost private consulting earnings. I wondered whether this level of dedication a prerequisite for later leadership. Accordingly, she has resorted to extreme levels of organisation in her life, to juggle the competing needs of being doctor, mother, wife, friend, sister, daughter, reader, gym-attender, gardener. And she freely admits it has taken its toll.

Christine: I have a lot of energy and can fit a lot into my day. I can burn the candle at both ends, and I've always hoped that by doing that I was compromising *myself* instead of anyone else. Particularly when my family was young, I felt very much that they had to be prioritised no matter what. What I tried to do was avoid working on weekends, to do all my work after they had gone to bed or before they got up in the morning and to really focus on their needs in their waking hours. I had a husband who was dedicated to caring for them and who was exemplary in the way he supported me. I spent a lot of money on long-distance phone calls, before we had mobiles. But I think the other compromise you feel as a working mother is that you can't go to all the things at school.

I think about it all the time. I don't know if a mother who's had a major career is ever able to say with total assurance and comfort to themselves, I did my best therefore do not feel bad, do not worry. I look back and wonder how it might have been for my children had I been more available immediately after school. We had wonderful people looking after our kids. We were

> willing to pay every cent of what I earned to achieve a good outcome. We gave everything we could to making sure they were well looked after, that they were at home, bathed, fed and had continuity. But I often think, what if I had been at home and they had come home to me every afternoon? Would that not have been better for them? I don't know the answer to that, but it does plague me a little bit. And yet our kids have turned out fabulously, well developed and wonderful in so many different ways.
>
> I do remember leaving Tim [her son, now thirty] a couple of times and just feeling a terrible anguish about it, and what I don't know is whether what I saw was the anguish in his face, and I certainly did see that a couple of times, or just what I felt in my own heart, which was awful. Leaving your children is a really uncomfortable feeling, deeply uncomfortable. What if I had done things differently?

We agreed that we won't really know what our children truly felt about our compromises till they start making some of their own decisions about children: whether they prioritise more uninterrupted time with them or whether they follow our lead. Maybe they did appreciate the vitality that parents' work brought into the household? Maybe they appreciated the money too.

I wonder whether Christine has experienced that fear of failure related to the 'imposter syndrome'. Very occasionally, in our long friendship, I have seen her pushed to the edge of her abilities. One incident especially made a huge impact on me. A young female patient presented at Concord Hospital's emergency department some years back. She was exceptionally ill with breathing difficulties, and she was deteriorating. She was admitted under Christine's care. Amid the family's growing alarm at their daughter's decline, Christine and her team attempted to work out what was wrong. But a clear diagnosis eluded them. Days passed without the source of the young woman's illness being identified. Copious pathology tests couldn't uncover the problem. Broad-spectrum drugs were used until a precise cause could be found. The tension was unbelievable while this young woman's life hung in the balance. Eventually, after about six days and a medical detective operation worthy of the best sleuths, an answer emerged. The appropriate drugs were administered and the patient was restored to her family within a few days. How does Christine manage when her skills appear to be insufficient?

> Christine: What I've always said to myself in these sorts of situations is, do you have the skills, do you have the physical wherewithal? When I've been on the edge it has been because I am dealing with an extremely difficult set of circumstances with a patient I've been very, very worried about. More often, very frequently, I am near to exhaustion, often because I've had too much to do and I've said yes to too many things, but I'm really unwilling to let myself think about that. At those times, I have said to myself, what could you have done better? Or I've even said to myself, it's okay, it's just that you've not yet learned to say no. That is a big weakness of mine.

In these big caring professions, the game is so obviously worth the effort, the striving so legitimate. Yet the system itself, secure in its identity, does not seem to have any doubts about whether its conventions—around hours spent at work, for example—are reasonable for certain groups, like mothers. I can see how a highly motivated, intelligent and ambitious woman like Dr Christine Jenkins, with a strong sense of duty and drive, is determined to keep pushing herself to explore what having authority in medicine and science means, personally and professionally. She acknowledges some concern, too, about the type of leadership she demonstrates, whether she might morph into a female version of the uber-powerful men.

> Christine: People have said to me, many times, that I have a natural authority. But I think you have to be very careful of it. At times I have been accused of being schoolmarmish! And perhaps that's one of the things you can evolve into, being a bit dogmatic or didactic or just forgetting that you're just an average Joe Blow person at times. I do feel I've evolved into having authority. I think it's a good thing to have, but it's very, very important not to be consumed by it or allow it to dictate the way you relate to people day by day. I think, in a way, it's something you keep in the cupboard and get it out when you need it but don't necessarily wear every day.

This accumulated authority—Christine is in her seventh decade—means she is now regularly offered to step further and further outside her comfort zone into exciting new fields. The latest instance is her work at Sydney's George Institute for Global Health, which involves huge research into interventions for China and other parts of Asia. She will be assessing more affordable interventions for COPD (chronic obstructive pulmonary disease) in more than thirty centres, pioneering a type of collaborative science between Australia and the Asian region that offers vast potential. She also belongs to several select international committees that ensure rigorous conduct of large global studies in lung disease, requiring exceptional clinical skills and commitment.

At Hornsby Girls High School, back in the 1960s, Christine's much-loved science teacher Joan Webb constantly encouraged her to consider as open a future as her imagination would allow. Christine remembers this as a thrilling, countercultural invitation. After all, her father, John, thought she should do an arts degree at university and enjoy lying round in the arts quadrangle between lectures! Girls who held Commonwealth scholarships, he contended, were wasting government money as they would just get married and never take up work in the professions.

Christine ignored his advice and took up Mrs Webb's suggestion to dream outside her boundaries. She found it very congenial. So she aimed high, to be a doctor, a specialist and a leader in her field, all far beyond her parents' imaginings. Risks and rewards have accompanied her, and some regrets and reservations. But she is a satisfied woman, enthralled with her work. It is hard to imagine her in any other realm. And she now passes on her teacher's enthusiasm to a new generation of young women, for whom it is not countercultural at all, in theory. But they have to live the dream, and if Christine's experience is any guide, it is still full of challenge.

CHAPTER 13

PRISCILLA COLLINS

Mothers Rule, OK

Priscilla Collins is an indigenous woman leader. She grew up and was educated in Alice Springs and became interested in television production. Priscilla began her career as a production assistant at the Central Australian Aboriginal Media Association (CAAMA) and went on to work for almost twenty years as a prize-winning filmmaker and administrator. She then decided to change course and take her organisational skills to the Northern Australian Aboriginal Justice Agency (NAAJA), where she now presides over the provision of broad-based legal and social services to the Northern Territory's Indigenous population.

FOOTY legend John Kennedy's famous 'don't think, do' mantra seems the best summary of what motivates one of the most comfortable women leaders I've come across. Priscilla Collins is the original den mother, with six children, all largely raised on her own, four grandkids and at least another four children from other mothers, mostly relatives. But then her definition of 'relative' is more fluid than that of most non-Indigenous Australians. Priscilla is an Indigenous woman from Alice Springs, who has now relocated to Darwin. She learned her formal skills in the television industry and has now moved on to what she calls 'the legal industry', where she is CEO of the North Australian Aboriginal Justice Agency. The NAAJA gives broad-based support to Indigenous people inside and outside jail.

Priscilla sees a seamless transition from helmsmanship within family life to leadership in the broader world. In her current role as head of the largest legal service in the Northern Territory, she oversees about 110 staff, sixty-five of whom are lawyers and fifty per cent of whom are Aboriginal. 'It's not rocket science, you know. You ask our mob on the ground, what do you need? And then it's my job to go out and find the money and get it put in place.'

That is classic Cilla. Things crop up. You work out what's needed and then act. You don't wring your hands. If you're criticised, you face your critics in person. You get on with it, even when tempted by despair.

> Priscilla: It's reality, I suppose. It's heartbreaking. You listen to some of the stories and it's just heartbreaking. But, you know, my thing is I just have to work out the best way I can to help. I'm not going to solve things overnight. I know that, but it's a step in the right direction and somebody's got to do it.
>
> Geraldine: You're a reactor, aren't you?
>
> Priscilla: I just go boom, full pelt ahead. I worry about it when I hit the other wall.
>
> Geraldine: Are you a planner?
>
> Priscilla: No, not a planner. What I'll do is listen. I'll sit in meetings and I'll listen to everything and then I'll pick up on things that I know I can do. Even though it can be pie-in-the-sky stuff, I'll jot down step by step how I think I can do it. Then I'll do it.
>
> Geraldine: I detect that you're not a bullshitter.
>
> Priscilla: I couldn't lie to someone, because I wouldn't be able to convince myself!

I love that observation. It goes hand in hand with the candid image Priscilla presented to interviewers when going for the job at NAAJA in 2007.

Priscilla: It was time to get out of Alice. It wasn't a good environment to raise my kids in and I'd just been through a nasty divorce and lost everything. So I came up to Darwin with no job, no house, no car, saw a job in the paper and went for it. It was a CEO position and the requirement was that I should have had a legal background. I went into the interview very clear and upfront with everyone on the panel and said, look, I have no legal background at all—I haven't even been inside a courthouse. You could just see their faces go, what? But, I said, I have great management skills, great governance skills and I know how to bring in money, and that's what I'll do for this organisation.

The figures say it all. The NAAJA budget was about $4 million, Priscilla says, when she started: now it's around $30 million, from various buckets of money. The NAAJA provides myriad services, ranging from the straight legal kind to night patrols, assisting the Royal Commission into child abuse, legal education, and cooperative research projects with the police. Priscilla has pioneered an MOU (memorandum of understanding) with the Department of Corrections allowing her staff to be based in the prisons. She claims that no other Australian jail has Aboriginal Legal Service staff based inside their walls.

Priscilla outlines all of this very matter of factly. It takes a little while to process the scale of the ambition and systematic follow-through of this Territory leader. But then I haven't met many women with a CV quite like Cilla's. She looks white (her father is white) but she comes from a 'big black family', as she puts it, from the Alice Springs town camps. She grew up out bush, heavily influenced by an impressive-sounding grandmother, an

East Aranda woman, who speaks fluent language even though she is a stolen generation child. Before she went to high school, Priscilla insists she didn't grasp any real difference between black and white, not until a white boy walked her home and gasped when he realised that 'her nanna was a boong!' Her sister would subsequently be called a 'gin' and her cousins 'coons', and, because Priscilla looked so white, her indignation at these offences confused all concerned.

> Priscilla: At Nanna's, everyone speaks language. We grew up poor, you know, we never had air-conditioning or heaters or running hot water. We never had flushing toilets. We had drop toilets out the back, so we grew up really, really poor. If we wanted food, we had to go out bush and get a killer or go get a nanny goat or go get a kangaroo. That's how we grew up.
>
> Geraldine: What's a killer?
>
> Priscilla: A bullock, a cow.
>
> Geraldine: So you slaughtered your food?
>
> Priscilla: Yeah, that's how we grew up. My nanna was the leader of everything, you know. She raised all her kids. All the family would come to my nanna's house. Nothing went past her without her approval, and I think I watched how she did it.

Priscilla did more than watch. From both her grandmother and her mother, she imbibed into her bones that sense of family responsibility, especially regarding younger members. She was next in the female line, so brothers, sisters, nieces, nephews, cousins all came under her wing. 'Was that a burden or a joy?' I asked. 'You just do it,' she said simply. And it was a very good life, she recollected, full of inventive playing and dance competitions and witchetty-grub hunts. Except for one terrible episode, the details of which tumbled out, unprompted. When she was seven, Priscilla was kidnapped by an itinerant white man from her busy camp home and taken to the nearby river. He tried to pour alcohol down her throat (she's never touched a drop since), tied her up and clearly planned awful deeds. Fortunately, she was rescued by her uncles and the police before terribly long.

> Priscilla: My parents must have realised I was missing because there were police cars driving up and down, so every time a police car would go past he had my hands tied behind my back and he would push my face into the sand so I couldn't scream or anything like that, and then I remember he must have been trying to have a drink or something and I got up and I ran, and as a little kid running through sand it's just like a nightmare, just hoping somebody's going to see you. Unfortunately, they didn't and he grabbed me and suffocated me again. And we were down there for quite a while and then we saw a flashlight coming, and then that's when all my uncles were there, all the other men were there, my dad. That's when they'd spotted him.

She understands he was well known to police for having offended against his own wife and children and was subsequently evicted from the Territory. More than that, she either doesn't know or doesn't care to tell me.

Whatever the deep impact of this incident, Priscilla didn't let it interrupt what she considered a normal path towards adulthood. What intrigued me was what it said about her resilience, which would buttress her then and now, and about her capacity to absorb trauma and yet disconnect herself, somehow, from it. By volunteering these details, which otherwise I'd never have known, she proved that she has never forgotten what happened. But it does not dominate her internal narrative. It is merely one episode in her complex, unfolding life.

This seems pretty healthy to me. However, Priscilla's life can't have been all smooth sailing. She moved out of home at sixteen, because there was just so much family around, all the time. She slept on people's lounges, in swags if necessary, and worked at Coles, service stations, anywhere, to support herself. Then her luck turned. Indigenous pride was on the rise, which led, thankfully, to some institution building. In 1980, the trailblazing Central Australian Aboriginal Media Association (CAAMA) was set up in Alice Springs as a hub for Aboriginal broadcast material. Priscilla joined, in its early years, as an administrative assistant. Knowing everyone and considering them virtually all family—she felt she'd raised many of them—it was an ideal fit.

> Priscilla: You know, you mention my name down there [in Alice Springs] and they go, oh, we remember, she used to have one baby on the front, one baby on the back, three in the pram, couple more hanging off the trolley. Everyone just saw me as this women who had a million kids. No one knew which were mine and which weren't!

Priscilla loved going to work. She'd work until up to an hour before going into each labour, and then bring the kids back to work. And in twenty years she climbed her way up through the ranks to become executive producer of documentaries and series and, eventually, to CEO. Being so closely connected to most of the staff, how did she manage the hard-nosed part of leadership?

Priscilla: I'm still that same Alice Springs black girl that everyone else would have grown up with. I still talk and act the same, and I am an honest person. So if I have to discipline someone, I'm not going to go in there and put on a different face. I just go in there and say, these are the facts: this is what you did wrong, and unfortunately because of what you've done wrong, you have to go.

Geraldine: And that doesn't give you palpitations in advance?

Priscilla: It's just what you have to do. Oh, look, when I started at NAAJA, I had the difficult job of having to do a whole restructure and really pull people into line, including board directors. Things just weren't happening, or people had been in positions for too long and weren't doing things. But no, I didn't feel guilty about anything, because I made sure I had all my facts to back me up. For example, I had to get rid of a staff member in Katherine who had been there for a very, very long time, but times had changed. The position wasn't warranted any more. I just had to get all my facts together so that I knew what I was doing and then meet him and say, look, that position's changed; we no longer need your services, but this is what we are going to do to help you out too, in your future. He wasn't happy. He had a lot of people in Katherine ringing me up.

Geraldine: No one threatened you?

Priscilla: Oh they did. They thought I was just a little white girl. I thought, I've got no problem, I'll drive to Katherine. Just bring them all in and I'll sit there. So I went down to Katherine and he brought all these male friends in, a lot older than me, and they said, who gives you the right to come here and start making all these decisions and getting rid of our friend ? And I said, okay, do you know who I am? And they said, no, you're some white city girl. I said, no, I'm not: you know my family in Katherine. I named all my family there. Yep, that's my uncle, I said, that's my auntie, that's my cousin: now do you know who I am? Okay, now, the reason I'm getting rid of this position is because of this, this and this. You understand that? Yep. Okay. We've got a deal here? Yep. Done, finished. I don't want to hear no more about it.

Geraldine: So you are a good conflict resolver?

Priscilla: Yeah. I will not go in unless I know the full story, then I'll make a good judgment, and I'm confident to go in and sort it out. I don't care if it's a man. Men don't scare me, you know. I come from a background of strong women and we've all always ruled the roost. If I have to confront ministers, I have no problem with doing that. If they shoot you down, you go, phew, mate, I've had worse than that—I've had kids screaming at me at home. This is nothing!

In fact Priscilla's domestic and professional lives have been inextricably intertwined in sometimes hilarious ways. Like the time she came up with a concept for a television series for the Disney Channel and Channel Nine based on twins. At the time she had twin daughters, which is bad luck in Indigenous culture. The plot centred on an Aboriginal woman whose twin daughters were separated at birth: one grows up out bush, one in the city. Then they meet each other at sixteen, switch places, and the fun begins.

Priscilla: I flew over to the Cannes Film Festival, and, as usual, I go there with my big tribe. I had four kids then, and was pregnant with number five and I took my mother as a babysitter and my niece tagged along for the trip. So we all went over to the Cannes Film Festival and had the best time. It was a bit of a shock going into the market, and every network that had anything to do with children's television was there, and I rocked up—pram, big mob of kids, floaties, towels—and they're like, what the hell is she doing? I said, it's all right, you'll get used to me. And so I pitched to Disney. I had number four with me. So I go in there, do my little pitch, and then something was going down my leg, and I thought, oh, please, please don't even tell me this is happening. He'd done a big shit and it went all down my leg. I was in the middle of the meeting with all the commissioning editors and I just stood up and said, oh, I'm just going to have to tell you my son has just shit all over me. I'm just going to use your toilet. I'll be back in five minutes! So I had to quickly wash him up and come back, and they gave me the money! Fine, no worries. And I produced and created that series. And everyone goes, oh, that's so good. And I'm thinking, mmm, I'm not quite sure whether they felt sorry for me or liked my story.

Geraldine: Doesn't matter.

Priscilla: Doesn't matter. I got the money. Then my next step was to get our own television station, because the difficulty was that every time you wanted to make a film you had to get a pre-sale from a broadcaster. So I thought, if we have our own network it will make it a lot easier.

We can just go to our own network to get our pre-sale, and then I can go to the Australian Film Commission and get some money. The minister of communications at that time [Daryl Williams] put out a feasibility study for an Aboriginal television station. And then Owen Cole, Rachel Perkins and I sat down and decided to get our own national television network up and running.

Geraldine: This became NITV (National Indigenous Television)?

Priscilla: Yes, we got $48 million from the government. We set up the board and then got [the veteran indigenous bureaucrat] Pat Turner as a CEO just to start the ball rolling. It was big. We were getting AFI nominations, and I was travelling all around the world, talking to people and going to markets and all that sort of stuff.

Geraldine: And you felt yourself growing, as a person?

Priscilla: I didn't think I was a big hero. It was something you just do.

Surely the Collins ego has a few more edges than this, I say to myself. Does she feel no permission from her community to express pride in her competence? For it clearly exists. Look at all this bureaucratic cleverness, for a start. Would it be perceived as too individualistic to spell it out? Did she think of herself as ambitious? And, while I don't completely believe her self-effacing statements, I do think that she believes that her status is not the main game. At the end of the day, she says, 'you come home to a tribe of kids'.

Priscilla: And, you know, you've just got to be Mum again and get back into the swing of cooking and cleaning, and then get up the next morning—with, say, two kids to get to childcare, three kids to get to school—and off you've got to go and do another film. After school you've got netball, basketball, soccer, athletics. So you're just like that all the time and that's just with my kids. Then I've got all the other kids I look after as well. So I don't get time to think about anything. You just do it and get it done. For me to read a newspaper is a bit of a luxury: you go to my house and I have ten newspapers sitting there. I'll get to that tomorrow, I say, because I just don't have time.

Considering Priscilla's considerable career in top-level management, I can't believe there hasn't been a tussle that has tested all her verities. And, sure enough, there has, but it wasn't quite what I had imagined. It was a struggle for control of her beloved CAAMA's future direction and it involved bringing down another woman in authority there. It was one of those classic contests where the new broom is convinced that wideranging culture change must be instigated and the existing employees, in this case Priscilla, sensed that the creative soul of the organisation was under threat. It became very nasty. Locks were changed. There were arguments over accountability of funds. The constitution was combed to ensure things were done by the book and out of the gaze of the media. Eventually, the more senior woman, the new CEO, was sacked; the board was divided, then resigned. And a whole new group was appointed. Huge disruption ensued, ending with Priscilla's ascension to the job, during what she describes as 'the most stressful time of my working life'.

Priscilla: It was a really bad time, and I didn't want to go in there as a bad person. But I'm just representing the staff;

I'm representing the members. This is what I've been asked to do. It puts you in a difficult situation.

Especially difficult if you become a key beneficiary of the turbulence. Priscilla doesn't like the idea—what woman does?—of being seen to play politics for the sake of it. Though machinations can't always be avoided. As all the chaos erupted, she resigned and got a job in regional development in government. But the CAAMA people pleaded with her to come back. Funding applications for the entire organisation needed to be submitted urgently (within twenty-four hours). The chief financial officer and senior managers had been sacked, there were no copies of anything prepared thus far, and a board director laid it on her: it's up to you now, Cilla. Her usual calmness, a huge leadership asset, came to the rescue.

Priscilla: I found whatever paperwork I could, like the last audit, to give me an idea of what the budget was. But I couldn't find any previous funding applications so we had to start everything from scratch. I had one day to do an application for the whole organisation. Owen Cole and I just sat there saying, what do you reckon about this? That sounds good, yeah that sounds good, hey? So we got it in and we got the money. I said, that's it. I've done my deed; I've resigned and I've got another job to go to. Then the board came back to me and said, can you take on the CEO job? It was a really stressful time.

I asked Priscilla about her experiences of racism, which I detected might have emboldened her. At one point, she applied for what she describes as a 'crummy little media advisory job', for which she was surely a legitimate candidate, having so much CAAMA experience under her belt. She had acknowledged her Aboriginality on the application form's nationality section. One of the young departmental workers rang her up and said, I'm just letting you know that you didn't get shortlisted for the interview and the reason is because you don't have enough experience.

Priscilla: She was really nasty to me on the phone, and I thought, you're treating me like a real 'black' aren't you—you're actually talking down to me like I'm a piece of shit. So I thought no worries, honey. Then the job came up for a director's position for the whole regional development thing in Central Australia—in other words, it was up there whereas that little media thing was down there. So I thought, I'm going to go for this job, just to prove a point. And I took my background off as being Aboriginal: I just put Australian. Got the job! So then I ring up this little girl and I said, honey, remember when you rang me and said I didn't have enough experience? And she says, yes, I did. I said, well I'm now your boss! I didn't end up taking the job—I went back to CAAMA—it was just to prove a point.

There are other stories like that. They bequeathed her a thicker skin, she says. But not in her personal life, oh no. There lies a great deal of heartache, which still has the capacity to sting. On the surface, she says, people saw hers as a glamorous life in the media world. At home, it was apparently a very different story, and her marriage ended, to her bitter regret. She took the five children and moved to Darwin, leaving all the rest behind. One more baby was born there.

Priscilla: I had to start from scratch again. I didn't even have a car. I had nothing at all. I had to work in Alice for another

> year so I could save up a bit of money just to get out of there. I moved up here [Darwin] with five kids and ten boxes. That was my life. No job. No house. No money. I was doing a bit of consulting work for Indigenous Business Australia and also NITV.

The NAAJA job came up, rounding off what she considers to be one of her most successful moves for her and her family. This year, her three daughters are at university, doing science, psychology and nursing, and one plays netball at national level. Her three boys live with her in Darwin. All her children have represented the Northern Territory in a range of sports: again, all these details are volunteered, as a badge of pride. They encapsulate what is, for her, a holistic story of leadership on her terms. And, like every Aboriginal leader I've ever met, she admits her work is more than a mere job.

The question of different expectations and styles of expression between Aboriginal and mainstream Australia is a delicate one, but it has always intrigued me. We can be too nervous to discuss it publicly. But by dodging it, by being coy, we might miss the opportunity to highlight particular aspects of leadership that are best suited to particular Indigenous community needs.

The veteran Aboriginal leader Mick Dodson told me during an ABC Radio National interview in the late 1990s that, for the next twenty-five years or so, most of the gains in Aboriginal Australia would result from small, not grand, gestures. Really, Priscilla Collins' achievements straddle both. For her, work provides that rare opportunity to shape better lives for her brothers and sisters, a higher purpose, but tiring for all that. Mobiles are never turned off. Complaints from her own mob are a given. Socialising after work is an optional extra that is usually sidelined. 'I go home to kids,' she says. I doubt this mothering manager will ever let it be otherwise.

CHAPTER 14

SIMONE WILKIE

A Tomboy Learns to Rule

Major General Simone Wilkie AM never intended to hold any position in the Australian Defence Forces, let alone one of such high office. She initially sought to become a physical education teacher, but through a series of accidental encounters, she joined the Australian army, where she thrived. Simone served in senior positions overseas and is now in charge of all training for the army as commander of the Australian Defence College.

IN my experience, people in the military are very serious about leadership. They believe profoundly that groups work only within clear lines of authority with specific duties even though good, modern militaries devolve that responsibility as far down the ranks as possible. I discovered a new phrase during my writing: the 'strategic private', a position even further down the hierarchy than the 'strategic sergeant'. These terms derive from the notion that the best decisions are those taken at levels closest to the action being experienced, an idea gathering strength in various arenas of modern life including business and the public service. The Australian armed forces pride themselves on training all ranks to take responsibility when necessary. Spotting those capable of leading others is core business. Questions of character are involved. After all, these leaders must be able to guide others under fire in war zones, where lives are at stake.

The classic image of the military leader has been male, with all those decorated generals dominating our imagination. But in the late twentieth and early twenty-first centuries determined agents of change, like Head of Army General David Morrison, came up through the ranks and the emphasis began to shift. Now there is a determined effort to broaden female representation in all ranks, including among senior officers, and to seek out the women who are comfortable to break those visible gender stereotypes.

It made me especially curious to meet one of the newest candidates, a woman who has risen from the bottom, with no specialist qualification such as engineer or doctor, to become a major general. Simone Wilkie is now in charge of all training at the Australian Defence College, the first woman to reach such a superior position. Hers is a feat to be celebrated. But I was also keen to discover how someone bucks the male leadership traditions that are so well established in the military. And, if women like her are tapped to rise up the ladder, how they then experiment with unfamiliar behaviour and psychologically reposition themselves to integrate leadership into their identity.

One of Ballarat's most famous exports, Simone wears her responsibilities pretty easily. This tall, strong-looking redhead with a steady gaze, rises to greet me in the ABC coffee shop. She exudes a natural confidence that I associate with authority (even though she's in civvies) and a keen intelligence. Not especially feminine in style, she declares before too long that she'd been a tomboy all her young life. She was surrounded by men. She had a younger brother, played lots of sport, and her father ran the university hostel, which was 'pretty male'. 'I found the femininity piece a little bit harder, to be honest.' Simone has wrestled long and hard with straddling that divide between being yourself and being what you think the culture around you wants you to be. She described this as the 'femininity tightrope' at a talk about the challenges women face when she was guest speaker at the Chief Executive Women's dinner in Sydney in September 2013. Because she's so clear-cut and self-aware, her advice is particularly helpful, in my view.

> Simone: I've found that if you act like a man, people will listen to you as a leader, but they are unlikely to respect you. Certainly, no one wins respect by trying to be one of the blokes. It is unnatural to try to be a bloke or, in fact, anything that you are not. It is important to remain a woman and not to underestimate the importance of self-esteem and self-confidence. When you have confidence in your ability, you can make the most of the opportunities when they are presented to you. Respect is a much more durable asset than popularity. Leaders who crave being liked generally fail—in their mission, and at being liked. There is no substitute for professional competence, and, in the army, that includes fitness and high personal standards, especially for women. You may not be the hardest in your team, but you must put in your best effort and show you are prepared to meet the standards you set others.
>
> I have learned that you need to be genuine and honest. Soldiers can sniff out lies at a hundred paces. You must be honest and expect it in return. Truth should not be taken as a personal insult. If you want soldiers' trust, you also have to make it known that you want people's opinions, not what you think you want to hear. You don't want yes-men—they can be incredibly dangerous.

You don't want to be one of the outsiders either, she acknowledges. It's tricky being one of a minority group, but Simone believes she has drawn on some key legacies from her upbringing in her rise as a leader. It helps, she believes, to have a sense of humour, and her father's rather democratic attitude: 'My father was incredibly adept at speaking to anyone. You never judge a book by its cover, he'd say, and I think that was an important thing that I grew up with.' Is Simone yet another female leader whose formation was dominated by a big father-figure? Well, not quite. Her mother, it turns out, is a strong, forceful woman, who encouraged her children to sample lots of different experiences, and who was a substantial figure in her daughter's growth. 'It certainly was never a case of "you can't do that",' said Simone.

John and Jean Burt, both teachers, knew that in their young daughter they had a 'big, strong-willed character' on their hands. Her mother's father, who'd been a Changi and Burma Railway PoW, used to call her 'the little red-headed bugger'—indicating a distinctive character above all! The challenge with such children is to harness that impetuosity rather than crush it. But the Burts were equal to the task of rearing her well. The whole household was devoted to sport, and Simone played in a large number of teams where she was invariably captain. Learning to play golf at the age of twelve taught her how to regulate her temperament, she says. Jean Burt kept her daughter fully occupied and worked hard on moderating Simone's forthrightness. 'She would say, Simone, you need to think before you connect your tongue! So over the years I've tried, and most of the time I succeed, but, still, I say things that probably would have been better not in my "outside voice".' She dwells on the nature of her communication with staff and is constantly monitoring whether she could do better—a key aspect of modern military management.

But Simone almost didn't make it into the military. She had

intended to be a phys-ed teacher and merely accompanied a teenage friend to the recruiting centre. There, she decided the army sounded like fun and put her own name down. Her father was happier for her to join the army than to teach because he thought it offered more opportunities. Not for the first time, he was right about his daughter. There's a lovely story about her parents' intervention around this time. A few months after signing up, the impulsive eighteen-year-old decided she'd been wrong, that the army wasn't for her. So she applied to resign. The Commanding Officer rang the Burt home in Ballarat to inform them that Simone had said she'd joined without sufficient thinking, without much research, and, realising she'd been incredibly naive, had chosen to get out.

> Simone: The CO said, we can send her back to Ballarat or keep her here in Mosman. To which Dad said, leave her there, she'll like it eventually.

And so she did, partly because she came to identify strongly with various individuals within the army. She was mightily influenced by a military legend when she became deputy chief of staff to General David Petraeus, commander of allied forces in the second Gulf War in Iraq and later commander of all Australian troops serving in that theatre. The American general was at the top of his game, sparking major changes in strategic direction and prioritising counterinsurgency, rather than the outright hostilities of the so-called Surge. Simone had to learn the American military's methods and sensibilities, which were rather different from Australia's. And she had to learn in the midst of complexity and, often, chaos. This was indeed stepping outside her comfort zone, just what the textbooks recommend.

> Simone: That was probably the most difficult, the most

challenging environment for me. When I arrived in Baghdad, I didn't quite understand the role I was going into. I was learning the American military language and also learning the diplomatic procedures, because the role I had as assistant chief of staff partly involved getting the military and diplomatic parts working together on a number of issues like the campaign plan. And they are totally different cultures in themselves. I'd describe the military as tending to be like scientists: there's a formula, there are different options, but you will get a solution. And the diplomatic element as more like artists: there are these factors, this and that, and eventually we might come to some answers, but then again maybe not. They're both interesting cultures and so it was good to learn to work around that. And we had a whole range of different countries each with its own approach to doing business. I found it fascinating. I think I learned a number of things about how to get to the word 'Yes'.

Geraldine: Did you learn to change a few of your rules there?

Simone: Well, actually, the Americans are more rule-based than the Australians. General Petraeus is a fascinating man. I'm sure he has a photographic memory. He was very good at explaining his intent. So every morning he'd give an update and we'd all get to see what he'd been briefed on. He'd stress specific points so that they would permeate down through the chain of command. It was quite clear what he expected and wanted.

What was the key lesson she took from this seminal experience? The answer was a surprise.

Simone: I used to follow all the rules. But I think I'm far more effective now. And that's another theory I have: that young women when they joined the military in the eighties would follow the rules far more religiously than the men did. Once they started to understand the system, they'd be more flexible with those rules. Over time, I have. Bill [her husband] says I don't actually think the rules apply to me! I take a slightly different approach: that there are some rules you absolutely must follow to the letter. But there are others that you should think about. Do we actually need that rule? Is it applicable for what we really need now? Should we be changing it or providing more opportunities for people to interpret the rule for their circumstances? I'm more inclined to say to people, that's not what I asked for and to be quite specific, rather than spelling out the rules. I follow the 'disappointed parent' approach, and I've got to tell you it works nearly every time.

Simone acknowledges that B-grade-movie depictions of the military have created impressions of soldiers having orders barked at them and being treated like cannon fodder. It's just not like that, she says. Tearing strips off people is bound to produce an unhappy result. She might still be obeyed, strictly speaking, but she might have angered her people, deep down: bad result.

Geraldine: So when things do go wrong and bad judgments have been made, how do you discipline people?

Simone: I always give people the opportunity to outline their approach—I learned that when I was younger. If you attack first to find out what happened, it's not such a good plan. And if they say, I did the wrong thing, well you instantly have a better relationship. If they're not stupid, and even if there are no mitigating circumstances, you end up with a much better outcome.

Geraldine: Do you allow people to make more than one mistake?

Simone: Oh yes. I adopt the approach, I trust you to do your job unless you prove to me otherwise, rather than, you have to earn my trust. I prefer to tell people what I'd like them to achieve and let them get on with it.

I was impressed at how Simone felt she faced a never-ending quest for improvement in her communication methods. She also offered some interesting hints for other women who are seeking to develop better skills.

Geraldine: What have you learned about how you communicate best and how you step back, even when you think you're right and others are wrong?

Simone: When I was younger, I was a lot more hard-nosed in my decision-making, and compromise wasn't necessarily something I could even spell correctly at the time. I learned that blowing up my bridges wasn't necessarily a good part of the plan. I'm a pretty easygoing person actually. We get an annual report, and regularly I've had comments about being 'refreshingly honest'. I think there's a balance between that and perhaps expressing everything you're thinking at the time.

Geraldine: In the civilian world, when people list qualities associated with good political leadership it's surprising the number of times that word 'wily' comes up. It can sound like a form of being two-faced and initially I didn't like that notion of leadership. But I've come to think that wily leaders are those who come through the middle and get outcomes that can be beneficial and change things… it's quite a skill. What do you think?

Simone: Yes, it's a way of massaging your way through to getting things done, which is the skill of leadership. It's about influencing people. That's why it's important to understand all the people you're working with and to acknowledge that everyone's different. As I've got older, I've become far more diplomatic in my dealings. I might still be saying the same thing, but I'll use slightly different language.

Geraldine: And you don't feel like you're being duplicitous?

Simone: No. I am still incredibly direct. If I need to cut to the chase to find out what's going on I will ask very directly. In fact, we had an incident last year and someone rang me to explain what had happened. After I hung up the phone, my husband said, boy, you grilled that bloke! You were really into him! It was just the manner in which you extracted the information. That was really good feedback for me. And I always think it's really important to have a close relationship with your partner because they will tell you the truth.

Articulating her values and expectations is a high-order issue for Simone, as a senior army commander. She has now dealt with thousands of recruits and has thought deeply about the patterns of compatibility and incompatibility within the army, as well as readiness for authority. Simone believes that the younger generation's relationship with technology affects whether they're well equipped for the army's collegiate environment. Even more, she thinks it influences their values, and not necessarily positively. Following the so-called Jedi council scandals (where a group of young Duntroon cadets filmed themselves having sex with fellow female cadets and then shared the images via mobile phones) within the army, it is not a big surprise to hear her views. It must be dispiriting for army supervisors when their presumed standards about good behaviour are so casually tossed aside by young recruits.

Simone: I have had a lot of experience with people who've recently joined the army. I'm pretty strong on the view that they have their own personal value system when they arrive. And so then it's our role to make sure that that system is aligned with our organisational values. In most cases, they are pretty closely aligned. And those with a rather large gap between what they've arrived with and what the organisation wants take more time to become culturally aligned. Or, they decide the army's not for them. It would be interesting to do a review to determine if, over time, that gap is bigger in our current society compared with the past. My gut feel is that it has become larger.

Geraldine: Is it, do you think, because there is more of a focus now on the individual rather than the group in society?

Simone: When I look at the training systems we go through quite often now, and in the last ten years, you're training a professional to go from selfish to selfless. And the critical piece of that revolves around their values and their understanding that they're part of a team. We have this saying in the army that there's no 'i' in team. That's why we spend a lot of time making people understand who they are and why they are here, and why they're responsible.

It all sounds very logical and inviting. But, to me, leadership, by definition, is pretty individualistic. Simone has to build the capacity for leadership in the midst of fostering teamwork. It can seem a tricky fit.

Simone: Everyone has their own unique leadership style. There are some fundamentals though. Education and experience are vital. You can learn from others' mistakes, but you tend to remember your own better. And, of course, there are different types of leadership in the defence space. There are times when you expect instinctive behaviour, so we'll go through a whole lot of training based on going on patrol in a war zone. I want to be able to give you some signals by hand, so you instinctively know what I mean and so that you do all the right drills instinctively if something goes wrong. That is specialised training: if this happens, do that! And then there are much broader parts of leadership. We have a concept called Commander's Intent: for instance, I might say, Geraldine, I'll meet you at the coffee shop about quarter past ten. And if you're not there by three minutes past ten, I'll know that you intend to be here soon. So I'll take what I think your intention is, and you effectively trust me to do whatever is required in preparation. So I use my initiative; I don't have to come back to you all the time to get further direction.

> But even when you train people in all these types of things, you have people on, say, the left side who just need a little bit of direction and then go off and do it. Yet on, say, the right-hand side, you'll have people with whom you have to be more prescriptive. I have to work that out even now with the staff who work for me: which ones need only a little bit of guidance and which need more specific guidance. I've worked with people who I have to have a little chat with…and they'll come back and need to have another chat with me to remember what I said. And then I'll need to write it down so that they can't misinterpret. You rarely get people quite like that but you have to adjust your style to get the best out of everyone.

Simone has had to grasp a few things that didn't come naturally. She survived the massive headlines when her then husband and ex-soldier Andrew Wilkie resigned dramatically from the Office of National Assessments in 2003 in protest against the Howard Government's actions in the Gulf War. As a serving officer throughout the drama, it can't have been easy. She has also realised that one thing she revels in, the physicality of the job, might be something not necessarily shared by her female compatriots and might inhibit many Australian women from considering an army career.

The Australian military is about eighty-five per cent male overall. The highest proportion of females serve in the navy (18.5 per cent), followed by the airforce (17 per cent) and the army (10.3 per cent). Women occupy only about three per cent of leadership roles at the moment.[11]

Simone: It's very difficult to attract women to a profession like the army. A lot more want to join the airforce. But I'd look back even further. A lot of girls by thirteen or fourteen start giving up sport. So they're not particularly fit. And the physical fitness requirements for the army are not easy. We've got to have this hurdle—if you don't have a high standard, recruits will get injured. We know that. So we've done all sorts of things like providing gym memberships and a range of other things to try to encourage the girls. I think that's one of our biggest challenges.

Then we have things like the Jedi Council! We also hear a lot about the work that [Sex Discrimination Commissioner] Liz Broderick has done. You know in your bones that people are saying, why would I send my daughter into that? But, actually, recruitment numbers have been great. I think part of that has been Dave Morrison—he's made a very positive change with his public statements, some of which have gone viral. But yes, we've still got misogynists in the military. We needed to have some people stand up and make it quite clear what won't be tolerated.

People are going to make mistakes. It's through the environment you provide that you aim to limit those mistakes. I would love there to be no more instances of sexual misconduct and a zero tolerance response. But I'm a realist. You look across society and people will do things that are unacceptable. I've had cases where I couldn't have made it any clearer what my expectations were, yet some people chose to do the wrong thing. I find that incredibly disappointing. When people come to work for me I'll say, these are my expectations. It's not a discovery tour, with you trying to work out my compass on things. We train people carefully. Some people, I suppose, will choose not to follow the rules.

Geraldine: What is the one thing you'd change to improve the situation of women in the military?

Simone: Volume. We simply need more women in the service. The opportunities are much greater than when I joined in the eighties.

When Simone joined the army as an eighteen-year-old in 1983, the thirty-two female recruits trained separately from the men. They learned how to fire weapons and about minor infantry tactics. But 'we weren't even allowed to do sword drill,' she noted. Of the thirty-two women, two or three are still serving thirty years on, and another bunch are still in the Reserves: a modest outcome. Simone joined the Signals Division (telecommunications), because women could only serve in units that weren't deployed overseas. It would have been unthinkable then that a quarter of a century later this same woman would be a brigadier in charge of the 1500 ADF troops embedded with international forces in Iraq's combat zones. It must have been quite a class, that year of '83. Another classmate is an ammunitions technician officer, who is brought in to disable explosives. Not many women gravitate to that work, according to Simone.

So, what about confronting a big fight with someone at work, the question that has provoked some surprising answers from other women in this book? Did she harbour some searing memory?

Simone: Well, I don't like losing. I think that's a strength and a weakness. If I think I have all the right grounds to contest, I will; in fact, sometimes I'll just argue the toss. And then people will say, you need to be careful about what you said then. And I'll just bark at them! On reflection, I think I might need to step back!

Geraldine: Well, quite a few of the women I interviewed did just that, often the night before the battle. Maybe they looked at the scale of the mess that could ensue, both for themselves and their groups. Perhaps they look at whether they're going to lose, and then draw back.

Simone: I probably do that on occasions. If some facts come to hand at the last minute. Or if I've sat down with other people and war-gamed the outcomes. I suspect part of it is that, in the military, we have what's called a 'military appreciation process'. We'll take a given problem, analyse what we want to achieve—what are the possible sources of action, what's the most likely outcome, what's the most dangerous and so on—and then work out which one we think will provide the best outcome, knowing what the risks are. So we've already weighed up the costs and all the factors that contribute to that decision. I've been trained to have an appreciation for problems. It really comes down to what risks are involved and the sorts of things associated with adverse risks.

Geraldine: Have you been in big competitive tussles?

Simone: I went through a big reform program four years ago when we were thinking about our training and education. And in my budget we had to save $100 million over ten years. It meant lots of challenges, but I saw lots of opportunities for the three services to be doing the

> same things, to pool our resources and come up with the future vision. So there was some competition, yes, but I also learned that if you're going to a meeting, it's better to resolve things before the meeting and not do it publicly. So, if I know you have a view that is divergent to mine, I'll probably have a chat to you beforehand.

Simone has become more strategic in other words. Maybe a solid dose of war-gaming could benefit many women. There's still much to come from Simone Wilkie, who is not yet fifty and who, due to her robustness and readiness to improve, will continue to grow as a leader. This is good news for the army and good for Australia. We will hear more of her, I feel sure, possibly much more. Hers is an interesting hybrid of independent spirit plus conformity to military rules plus high emotional intelligence, the capacity to reflect on one's behaviour on the run. It is a valuable troika of personal assets and so gratifying that traditional institutions like the army can now spot it. If she represents the new Australian approach to tapping women's potential, the future looks more promising.

CHAPTER 15

OTHER VIEWS OF THE CLIMB

'Everyone wants the job...not everyone wants to do the job.'

ALAN MOSS, former CEO of the Macquarie Group

'Women are in heated agreement about what needs to be done but it can't be done by women alone. (Gender diversity) won't happen without the ongoing commitment of powerful men.'

ELIZABETH BRODERICK, Australia's Sex Discrimination Commissioner, at a launch of the expanded Male Champions of Change network, 7 November 2013

'I've realised now that there's a whole lot of women whom I didn't find attractive in that particular way, whom I now realise are fabulous companions or whatever, and I realised that while my hormones were raging one way or the other, I've had a lifetime of simply not seeing a particular raft of women.'

DUSTIN HOFFMAN, at the age of sixty-one

MY intention in writing this book was to showcase an impressive group of women who were holding leadership positions in various Australian settings, in the hope of encouraging others to emulate them. I've always favoured stories of competence over lists of problems, so I wanted to hear the tales of achievers' lives, of their climbs. I wanted a chance to celebrate women who were performing to their full potential, rather than being hobbled by structural disadvantages or outright prejudice or their own sense of glass ceilings. Highlighting narratives of success can be a powerful motivator of others.

But I was also keen to round out this exploration of what I hope will be a new era for women by going one step further: by tapping the insights of some current incumbents of power and influence, the majority holders, who are men. From the start of my journalistic career, the people who controlled my newsrooms were mostly men. Only in the latter part of my career have I been subject to female leaders, but not one has ever been in the top job. So I have become very accustomed to observing the various approaches of powerful men; and I've come to believe that their wisdom can be extremely useful to aspiring women.

Powerful men can help develop road maps for would-be female leaders, whether or not they deliver their signposts in ways that we women necessarily like. It doesn't make those signposts wrong, just challenging. Disappointingly, they are often accurate in their portrayal of the difficult issues still to be resolved. I sense that many men are either no longer asked for public critiques of the women around them, or don't want to be seen to be passing judgment for fear of not appearing on-side.

Some criticism from men can amount to a defence of a male patch, as Nancy Milne pointed out, regarding some male whingeing about fewer board appointments available for those not wearing skirts. And some criticism, or supposed advice, can be gratuitously tough or patronising, as Ann Sherry experienced. But distinguishing between constructive criticism and self-serving slights is pretty easy to do, in my view. To eschew the perspectives of men who've succeeded partly because they can spot and then adapt to changing community trends ahead of others is to kick something of an own goal. After all, several of the women interviewed for this book, in particular Sandra Harding, attributed their rise in part to significant male mentors, whose generosity in handing on their experience of life near the top had been invaluable.

I sought out men I respected and who were prepared to offer their views about women acquiring or being denied, authority. I was keen to see if they'd been surprised by the fate of women who'd stalled or, alternatively, thrived within their sectors? Could they identify any patterns? How much did they think gender determined position in the hierarchy?

Each of these men had navigated public success and the challenges of governing others. All were keen to see more diversity among Australia's executive ranks and in leadership positions. But they weren't dewy-eyed about the realities of pushing what, to many people, is akin to our own cultural revolution. They were well aware of the pitfalls involved in acquiring power, strikingly so. Having been there and done that—or still right in the middle of it—they were acutely conscious of what success asks of people. Probably more than most, they're also alert to the sheer intensity of the modern workplace, especially in CBDs and among the uber-ambitious. In some cases, the men were actively engaged in boosting the rise of women. That often meant presiding over structural change to longstanding company conventions combined with a conscious, ongoing investment in key women. It was significant activity, but we can't yet judge their overall success and potential sustainability: the results are simply not yet fully in.

This chapter presents nothing like an exhaustive overview of men and women in senior executive positions. The material produced by the Champions of Change group, sponsored by Australia's Sex Discrimination Commissioner, Liz Broderick, provides that level of depth analysis and is discussed further in chapter 16. But the interviews with the nine men do provide a snapshot of perceptions about gender and authority across various arenas of Australian life at this point in our history—in politics, business, public service, the military and boardrooms. When I compare the men's views with the women's observations of their own lives, I find both overlap and dissonance. The men,

I suspect, might be surprised that aggressive tactics shocked some of the women and at their diffidence about entering very big fights. Some of the men's observations will console women: Lieutenant General David Morrison and Telstra's David Thodey reveal how they changed their minds about admitting more women and then altered their decision-making to provide opportunities. John Colvin, from the Australian Institute of Company Directors, was in the unlikely hero category. He converted his sense of initial helplessness about female advancement into bold, new action, which seems to have increased the numbers of women on boards.

Broadly speaking, the men were intrigued by questions of leadership identity and whether candidates could demonstrate the robustness required to manage high levels of pressure. But they were divided about how much gender itself was an issue. Most were curious about the possibility that women as leaders faced challenges different from those that men faced; by the same token, they were anxious that it was not overstated as an issue. Some wanted to emphasise the organisational changes required to enable a wider group, including women, to join in better. Others were fascinated by the different tone brought by women to committee work and negotiations, a tone they liked.

The head of the ABC, Mark Scott, tells an amusing story about being forced by his wife, Briony, a leading educationalist and principal of a major independent girls' school, to face facts about one of the differences between men and women at work.

> Mark: I do remember the phone call that arrived here one day, quite brief, in which Briony said, I just want to know, do you ever go to work and feel guilty? And I said, no, not really. She went on: do you know any men who go to

work and feel guilty? And I said, tentatively, I'm not sure.

Geraldine: And you started to realise you were entering dangerous territory.

Mark: She said, I feel guilty today [over family organisation issues]. I learnt a lot from that because even though I'm quite involved with our kids and try to be flexible where I can, perhaps men have largely escaped to the office. However, it's not quite as simple as that. I look at the women I work with in quite senior positions and often feel that they are dealing with a complexity of life that I don't actually see paralleled in the men who work in those roles.

Geraldine: What do you do with that conclusion, as a chief executive? It could hobble you, couldn't it? You could see hiring women as a problem. Or have you learned to trust that they'll absorb this extra load?

Mark: Well, I think what you've really got to try to do is have some emotional intelligence, some level of deep empathy that goes beyond the issue of the day and the issue of the moment. I don't think gender plays strongly in my mind, but I sometimes think you need to cultivate a sense that there is more going on than just the issue at the table, and that people are juggling different things. Four of our five content areas are run by women. I think they have more issues at play than the men do. But, going back to Briony's 'are you guilty?' question, I think there are more times when women of this generation pause and think: is this worth it? Surely there is another way. I think a number of women on the executive here in their forties and early fifties are thinking, maybe there are other things to do, whereas the blokes are still charging on through their careers.

Geraldine: I wonder whether men who get to those high positions—and maybe some female achievers like Gail Kelly, head of Westpac, for instance—learn to quarantine their lives, that somehow they don't invest as much in those family details, that there's not as much at stake for them?

Mark: I don't know, that's a really good question. I don't want to give the impression that women bring all their personal lives to the executive table, not at all. In fact, I sometimes quite deliberately ask about their kids or what's going on. One of my executives has a six-year-old, a three-year-old and a one-year-old and she is still breastfeeding—now that's a level of complexity that another member of the executive, whose youngest child is eighteen, does not have. What I've seen in her though is great focus and an ability to go beyond multi-tasking and focus with intensity.

Judging people by their longer-term achievements rather than their short-term dilemmas is very important, according to Mark. He believes that helping people to problem-solve is key. The one thing he simply won't allow, again influenced by his wife, is women 'arguing for their limitations', as she so brilliantly puts it, having seen women do it several times during job interviews for school positions. He's seen it happen too, and now tries hard to head it off.

This theme of brittle female self-esteem was picked up by Michael Deegan, a veteran public servant and head of

Infra-structure Australia till his resignation early in 2014. He senses that men who wish to help women's rise need to grasp the questions women constantly ask themselves: am I good enough? Should I be here? This questioning can be a double-edged sword, he says, because this reflection can be a strength.

Michael: You do worry about that lack of self-confidence, that introspection. Then again, women are always testing themselves, always thinking perhaps of how to handle something differently. I've worked with a number of female political leaders, business leaders and union leaders and seen different elements in them all. Their vision was a lot deeper and more generous than that of the men, who tend to focus on their own business silo. The women's introspection does almost hold them back. When women are included in the dialogues and the debates, they are really good, but it's getting the invitation that's the issue.

The different nuances and techniques that women could bring to discussions, particularly on issues in dispute, was highlighted by the former independent member for New England in the House of Representatives, Tony Windsor. He experienced the Gillard government's tumultuous years in Canberra and had something of a front-row seat as one of those who held the balance of power.

Tony: I found that women tend to think things through more, whereas men tend to make things more personal, especially if they find they're not beating someone. Women are more consensual; they listen well in committees. They consider their answers and don't automatically lace them with personal stuff. It helps to believe in something, it must be said. The magic ingredient is to be yourself. The punters are smarter than you think. They can sense if someone is true, and I think women are better at that, and they're far more considered in prioritising the issues.

He said he sometimes looked across the chamber at rising talents like deputy Labor leader and former minister for health Tania Plibersek with slight dismay because she was clearly not comfortable with the 'kill your opponent', two dogs in a prize-fight, strategy. Don't do it, he'd try to project across to her: it's not you and, frankly, you don't do it well.

Of course, the federal parliament's manners and mores have been under particularly close scrutiny ever since a woman became prime minister. But veterans of our systems, both state, federal and local, like the former Sydney Lord Mayor and Labor state minister Frank Sartor, reminded me that Australian politics is often exceptionally personal, both for men and women. Max Walsh, the respected political and financial journalist and commentator, offered the same insight. Both Frank and Max said that only women who could deal with what they called the messier end of the business and the tough tactics involved had a hope of surviving. Sartor is a veteran of various political bearpits: he headed the City of Sydney during the 2000 Olympics and was minister for planning under the Carr and Kenneally New South Wales Labor governments (2009–11). And he tussled with disgraced ex-colleagues Eddie Obeid and Ian Macdonald, who have been at the centre of explosive corruption inquiries throughout 2013 and 2014, among others. He has seen it all, as they say, fielding sentiments about his kids 'rotting in hell' and others wishing that he'd 'die a long and lingering death'. He smiles wryly these days when talking about these pressures, but they have clearly left their scars. And he was known as one of the more savvy political operators. The point is, this is not just handed out to women, he emphasises. Even Australia's political legends have copped it.

> Frank: They were pretty nasty to Howard; they were pretty nasty to Keating. I've had some horrible stuff—people can be vicious and very cutting and nasty. In Gillard's case it was sexist, yes. But if it had not been sexist, it would probably still have been pretty nasty. So is the sexism just a convenient outlet for people who want to be nasty? It may not be the cause of people's dislike of her, but the dislike manifested itself in a sexist way. So that's a society problem because it means we're using sexual labels to discredit people. Let's just say for a minute that none of the critics were sexist, they would have done a whole lot of vicious stuff anyway…see what I'm saying?

I think this explanation too easily dodges key issues which matter beyond politics. The sheer amount of sexist material that proliferated during the Gillard leadership, and its increased vulgarity, seemed to encourage people to become progressively disinhibited about the material or jokes they assembled. It was as if people came to believe that a different class of person was involved in politics—the political animal—and should they be caught in the crosshairs of a campaign, there was no real casualty because this wasn't a person with recognisable feelings. It seemed to me to be a classic case of dehumanising, which can usher in true horror if taken to an extreme. Commentators tried to trump each other with awfulness in what I saw as an essentially masculine contest, though I concede both men and women were involved. Rules of etiquette were there to be broken—that seemed to be the working principle—and it was all sanctioned by the notion that this was good, clean fun within a robust, political game. In my view, it seriously coarsened our national conversation and diminished our democracy. It stunned many women. If they were to put their hand up for public office, was this what they could expect?

Max Walsh told me he was horrified by the relentless attacks on Julia Gillard, even though he has become inured to the very personal assaults on people who take on public life. At the same time, he believed Gillard didn't know how to consolidate her legitimacy once she was in the top chair.

> Geraldine: What about that eruption of her anger that was so vivid in the famous misogyny speech among others: do you think, as some do, that that was a minus for overall female advancement, that expression of visceral anger?
>
> Max: No, at the time I thought: go for it, lady. She'd had a really rough trot. But look, if you get into the game, that's the way politics is played in this country, always has been...you've just got to develop a carapace and take it.
>
> The person who took stuff on the chin was Howard. He just absorbed it, but he never forgot one comment, by the way. Compare that with Julia and how she behaved, and she comes off second best. I don't think she was equipped for it. It disappointed me because when she got the job I thought she was. But the truth was she'd exhausted all her energies getting to the top. And while she was a narrow careerist in terms of getting to the top, she wasn't a professional careerist in terms of equipping herself for what would be called for in that office.

In this conclusion I hear stark echoes of what all the research suggests: that moving into leadership positions requires a fundamental repositioning of people's sense of themselves, which is easier said than done. It's interesting to reflect on how very few of the women I interviewed volunteered details of this personal metamorphosis, which is not to say it didn't happen. But I think their evolution had happened years before and they'd more or less forgotten about their approach prior to attaining leadership. In a way, this was consoling. It suggests, as Sue Morphet described the process, that cometh the challenge, cometh the woman, who then simply sees herself in a new light.

I don't think we can avoid the question of sexuality in the middle of all this. It is a tricky area and I approach it tentatively. But there are those women whom I'd describe as actively sexy, who give off an aura of desirability. And I have long wondered whether women perceived to be in their prime, so to speak, are really permitted to thrive when leading others. Would a female version of the sybaritic Bill Clinton (if such a person existed) be permitted to reign, even if she was as talented? Or would she be seen as just too threatening, with all that charm and barely concealed seductive power? Angela Merkel, Hillary Clinton and Janet Yellen are all highly successful, certainly, but with a contained sexual expression. Women like Christine Lagarde, even Margaret Thatcher, are hybrid figures, shall we say. Former New South Wales premier Kristina Keneally, a younger highly attractive woman, was possibly the first such example of outright sexiness I had ever seen succeed.

Seductiveness is clearly part of the armoury of public success: but how much of it is allowed for women?

Frank: Even if people think a woman is attractive, it doesn't necessarily mean they're going to vote for her. Julia was a very interesting cross. I think her spiciness both aroused some men, you know, and turned them off—it was really complicated. And, of course, when she was in parliament, she was on fire and I do think that led some people to do some very strange things, like the cartoons by Larry [Pickering, believed responsible for some of the more egregious graphic representations of her]. And there was that terrible thing that was on the ABC, that series about being in the Lodge [*At Home with Julia*]. Actually I thought that was appalling. If I'd been Mark Scott, I would have killed that. It was disrespectful.

Michael: I used to watch, in Canberra in particular, as the more attractive women would be invited to the meetings. The more capable women were left to do the work, and sometimes there was a crossover. Attractive women are capable, of course. But a couple of times I actually said to the people I reported to, no, I'm going to bring so and so in because she's bloody good at what she does, really extraordinary. Maybe it happens with men too, I don't know, but with the women it breaks my heart that people who really have got the right skill sets don't get recognised.

The former New South Wales Liberal premier and now ubiquitous board member Nick Greiner had a very interesting take. He senses that the women who succeed at very high levels on boards and in the CBDs don't define themselves as women. What on earth did he mean? Even more provocatively, he suggested that had Julia Gillard been opposed by, say, Malcolm Turnbull rather than Tony Abbott, the whole setting of the so-called misogyny debate would have been different.

Nick: If Julia had been opposed by Malcolm, if he'd stayed as leader, which he was just one vote from doing, it's interesting to consider what might have happened. I don't think there would have been a 'misogyny' debate. Malcolm would have said mostly similar things about her competence and breaking promises about tax, to what Tony did, but the impression would have been different. Even a Brendan Nelson or a Joe Hockey opposite her would have been different. It's worth thinking about. How different exactly I don't know, but you can bet your booties that it would have been really different even if Julia was the same person, did the same things, broke the same promises, you know everything was the same, except Turnbull had got one extra vote.

Geraldine: Because Tony appeared to be the archetypal male?

Nick: Yes, so it was the obvious stark contrast with her, this first female leader, and party politics was seen through conflict and a lot of this was Tony's choosing. But just by looking at them, the contrast was clear.

Maybe he's right in that the resulting debates activated archetypes that tapped deep, subliminal responses that lie in wait within us all, but which are rarely brought out into the light and tested. It was an intriguing thought.

Nick Greiner's observations arise from years of diving deep into the mysteries of boardroom conduct. He sits on nine boards and eighteen months ago was recruited by the Australian Institute of Company Directors as part of their big push for senior male executives to mentor female wannabes. He is mentoring three women at the moment. He knows that his ideas about a gender-neutral style aren't likely to appeal to me or to other women. Still, when asked to consider what marks the women who thrive from those who stall, my essential question, he reiterates his observations.

> Nick: Neuter is a good style. With men it's also true, because some are very male, in both politics and business: they're very gung-ho, they use a macho range of words…I don't really like working with those sort of men either. Others are more neutral. I think the whole debate is better through a neutral prism.

It's an interesting notion, but I don't think he's describing a level playing field here. I believe men are permitted to display a much wider temperamental range on the spectrum of hard driving to neutral than their female equivalents are. Colourful male personality types may attract attention in the gossip columns, but these characteristics are seen as part of the territory of creativity, a virtue. On the other hand, Sandra Levy discovered just how difficult these traits could be to work with day to day. And the description of her in the press as the ABC's dragon lady trumps any epithet I've noticed about men, despite some of their 'adventures'. On the other hand, one of Nancy Milne's assets, I suspect, is her grasp of that neutral tone that Nick Greiner prizes. Is it too high a price to pay for a seat at top tables? Is it too much of a compromise of self? Clearly Nancy thinks not, but it would be nice to think that in the near future, women not quite as disciplined as Nancy could still hope to contribute their talents usefully.

The hard-headed among us would say that structural changes, not those of role behaviour, are what are primarily needed to improve matters. Some big change-agents exist among key Australian male leaders at the moment. The Champions of Change group and the Australian Institute of Company Directors seem to be tackling things in a more systematic way than I've ever seen before. It is still too early to start popping the champagne corks, but there are some promising signs that influential men no longer think that achieving more diverse workplaces is easy, but that such workplaces will only follow deep reflection about unintended handicaps combined with bold tactics from the top down. The institute's director, John Colvin, is ecstatic about the latest results (June 2014) on the eve of International Women's Day. The total number of female directorships on ASX200 boards had more than doubled from 8.3 per cent in 2010 to 18.2 per cent in 2014. The number of ASX200 boards with no female directors had more than halved from eighty-seven in June 2010 to forty-two now. And the percentage of women among appointments to the top 200 company boards increased from 5 per cent in 2009 to 22 per cent in 2013. Female chairs had also doubled from five in 2010 to ten in 2014.[12]

These results didn't just emerge like magic. Former lawyer John Colvin says they were the result of a timely chairmen's mentoring program developed three years ago by the AICD, in an act of near desperation.

> John: We invented it, this program that's now so successful. When I came into the job [from a legal career] in 2009, women made up just eight per cent of board members on the top 200 boards. What could we do to move things, I thought. I rang every director in the Top 100 and said,

I want you to mentor someone. And I got fifty-six to say yes in that first year! They said to me, where are you going to get all the women from, John? Well, we got them. And we shifted the dial, because it turned things from being a political issue into a professional one.

This is smart thinking. It satisfies exactly that finding of the McKinsey research about identifying newcomers' needs in relation to those of the wider entity, rather than hothousing the newbies.[13] The institute also offers a board-ready program together with its Board Diversity Scholarship program. More than a quarter of the female appointments to Australian companies over the past four years are past or current mentees of the chairmen's mentoring group, claims a proud Colvin. Many of the scholarship-program participants have also gained directorships on listed company boards and in the not-for-profit and public sectors. Reading their material, I find that a lot of practical advice is being provided by the powerful for the less powerful. This includes the way CVs are structured, because women often need to summarise better the 'value proposition' they represent to a modern boardroom, as John puts it. Colvin's enthusiasm made me smile. He was so proud of making a difference because he once doubted that he ever could. As for those who do well on boards versus those who don't, after years of watching both good and dysfunctional boards at work, he felt there were some big questions of character involved.

John: You have to have courage: you have to be prepared not just to sit back and be passive if you're not happy with the ethical position of the listed company. You have to be brave, re-evaluate your thoughts, check your facts, listen and, if necessary, argue. You have to leave your day-job role and step into being a director. You do need to ask yourself, will I add value? That's for women and men alike, especially in public-sector roles, which can be quite political.

Lieutenant General David Morrison, Chief of Army, and Telstra CEO, David Thodey, have both had their road-to-Damascus conversions, it seems, over the last three to five years. In their different realms, they have become committed to shifting the goalposts. The general's appearances on YouTube and at the recent Angelina Jolie conference on violence against women have given him international star status. Both these leaders stress the need for flexibility at work and, in the army's case, to no loss of rank following maternity leave. For Lieutenant General Morrison, this was an epic shift. In an organisation with such a strict hierarchy, the decision to take time out to care for young children often stymied women's advance. They lost their place in the job queue. So, in the past, it often became for women a choice between children and career. Morrison saw this as an intolerable outcome and was determined to change the pattern.

David: The rates of singleness and childlessness in this newer generation of women are almost diametrically opposite to those of the women before them. We've put so much more effort into trying to understand female soldiers' needs and into gender-diverse efforts. We do have women becoming much more successful and being seen to be so. They're acting as role models. In fact, I have come to believe that the sorts of experiences they have being mothers is of real benefit to their role in the army, so they shouldn't be penalised for stepping out. There really does have to be a systematic and deep cultural response from the army, because these are

> broad, community, cultural issues at stake. In too many cases, a team has defined itself through the exclusion of women. But what we are saying as an organisation is that we are doing great harm to it by holding onto these tenets. We have a lot of conversations with young men and it is terrific to see them nod approvingly when some point is made about the place of women. I think it works best when the genders are combined. But I'll tell you this: we have not wasted a good crisis!

He is referring to the repeated incidents of sexual misbehaviour and coercion in the military, the sort that produce strident headlines and debate. It certainly ignites his passion, as his hugely viewed YouTube video condemning soldiers standards' of behaviour aptly shows. But he's also heartened by other figures from within the army. After publicly announcing that he wanted to see the numbers of female soldiers rise, and by introducing measures like the Join with a Friend program, he now boasts an eighty-four per cent increase in the numbers of new female recruits. The challenge now is to keep them.

Telstra's chief David Thodey is convinced that flexibility will be the determinant of whether women thrive or stall in the communications behemoth. 'All Roles Flex' is the overarching title of a new program providing that flexibility. Any manager who says it can't be done is asked: if not, why not? Thodey clearly has that quiet way of insisting that he be heard in culture-change overtures. It suits his plan for the company. He sees a lot at stake.

> David: Flexibility will mean different things to different people. For example, it may mean part-time work, or the ability to work certain scheduled shifts, or working

> different hours or at different locations. What I really like about this approach is that it disrupts the status quo and encourages open conversations right from the start. It empowers people to speak up and discuss how they can make their work and career ambitions fit with their life stage and commitments outside of work. This initiative evolved from a pilot program in our Customer Sales and Service team, which saw the number of women in the applicant pool grow by more than fifteen per cent and the share of women in job placements increase by thirty-five per cent, when roles were advertised as flexible.

Max Walsh had one final insight that came as quite a surprise about structures in our workforce. In the wilder 1970s and '80s, when he, as editor, and his deputy Fred Brenchley were early change agents at the fledgling *Australian Financial Review*, Walsh was specifically authorised to change the journalistic appointments policy. He was given permission to not only appoint women, but go outside the status quo among personnel dominated by the usual big independent schools. So he did just that, happily appointing mavericks, Catholics, ambitious women and people who were prepared to freelance a bit—that is, step outside the rules to get their stories. The women worked harder, it was as simple as that, he claims. Men were not as competitive, having had 'a sweet life'. The rest is history: with its new complement of staff, the daily *Fin Review* became required reading as the Australian economy lurched into its massive reform era.

But a hard-driving newspaper with ambitious plans to set new agendas clearly favoured driven personalities, male and female. Max has been fascinated by a different culture within the world of finance, a generation further on. The rules and regulations of the modern superannuation industry, where he now works as a principal with Dixon Advisory, suit women well, he believes. He feels that women are far more regulation-friendly than men. Women see regulations as a welcome guide, offering a certain security. Maybe the men, having been the dominant species, he speculated, did not appreciate what amounted to a new supervisor, in terms of strict regulations and oversight by government regulators.

I have come to a similar view, divined over years of watching well-run and less well run newsrooms. Women don't thrive in chaos, where the power relations are constantly shifting and where you never know when you walk out the door in the morning what you'll return to in the afternoon. I've been there and done that, and I didn't enjoy it one bit. But the superannuation industry, the custodian of Australian retirement funds, cannot tolerate anything like this lack of order. And a lot of women are doing very well in the super field. It hadn't dawned on me until now to see the parallel with regulation.

Max: Yes, the nature of the business requires that you have oversight and pretty strict rules to make sure that no one walks out the door with all the money. It breeds a particular attitude. Everyone knows that everything is cross-checked. This doesn't affect people in any adverse way. But it certainly makes for an entirely different atmosphere.

Geraldine: So might a more conventional, more conformist type of person come through? Not an outlier, not a radical.

Max: Oh, that's quite true. Our investment advice style is pretty rigorous. If you come in, we take your particulars and slot you into a particular area and this is what we recommend according to your age, taste, disposition to risk and so on. The point is that you can't go off the reservation, as an advisor. That suits women!

Geraldine: Because it doesn't really favour mavericks?

Max: No, not at all. Clearly there are some people in the broader finance industry who are quite idiosyncratic. I meet them from time to time, but we're in another sphere of influence and I don't have to deal with them. But for me, at this late stage in my career, it was quite a change to see an operation like this on the ground, to see how much more disciplined it was [compared with the media]. I think it favours women more than other occupations do. I think it will suit them a lot better than it does a lot of men. There's a lot of testosterone in the world of finance and some men are wild when it comes to investing.

Geraldine: Whereas everyone's hemmed in everywhere with superannuation. Thank goodness, I'd add.

Max: Yes, and it gives women comfort.

These men of power and influence have proffered a varied road map for aspiring women. Some of the observations, I know, will be immensely challenging. It will be proof to some women that they are playing with loaded dice, that the odds of real change are stacked against them and that they court ongoing demoralisation. It may be better not to tilt at that goal, they might say. But, wearing my optimist's hat, I choose to extract considerably more hope than despair from these accounts. Even if half the plans come off, the going could definitely get easier for women. But they will have to opt in and take the risk of accepting invitations to govern their space. Then they will have to do their best and enjoy the climb.

CHAPTER 16

THE BIGGER PICTURE

THE stories of the fourteen women included in this book emphasise authentic Australian lives with their highs and lows, their dilemmas and their achievements. But how do they fit in the broader landscape? I needed to equip myself with the latest research on women, here and elsewhere, to position us within the international context. What are the overall patterns for leadership aspirants in countries with whom we usually compare ourselves: where are women on the rise, where are they plateauing? Do their experiences echo the stories of the women I spoke to? Does the best research offer hints to those of us mulling over our fate and that of our work environments? Was there any genuine progress? I found there definitely was. The researchers didn't gild the lily but, overall, they were hopeful that attitudes towards female leaders were slowly becoming more accepting, even welcoming. The research was quite specific too.

The findings outlined behaviours that I think many of us will recognise. I learned a lot and consequently decided that this final chapter ought to summarise and disseminate those key findings.

In the past five to ten years, newspapers and financial magazines have devoted quite a bit of space to stand-out women leaders. The stories are generally gratifying, if you like tales of new entrants flourishing as leaders. But just as I discovered during my interviews with men, there's some coyness in naming outstanding difficulties, lest it seem counterproductive. It was gratifying that the best research highlighted some continuing challenges in terms of women's own attitudes and, even more, identified the gap between their approach and the existing conventions at work. It wasn't a case of saying one approach was right and another wrong, but, in trying to understand the status quo, good questions were asked about who thrived and why, who didn't and how that could change while maximising productivity. Some of the anecdotal evidence about workplaces is more bracing, it must be acknowledged. For instance, Sallie Krawcheck, the former Bank of America and Citigroup executive, recently claimed in the US business press that senior US women had actually gone *backwards* post-GFC, because men tended to hire people like themselves in a crisis. 'What I saw when I was on Wall Street is not, "let's get rid of people who are different to us because they've got cooties", but more, "yeah, I know diversity adds to business results in theory, but we are in crisis mode and I need that person who I can trust today".' she told Bloomberg.[14] Nevertheless, I am sure the research findings overall throw some light onto some of the obvious and the more subtle corners of modern workplaces and help both women and the men who seek to advance to leadership positions.

The most insightful research, I found, has been conducted

in the United States, primarily by the McKinsey Group, but also in France by the management training centre INSEAD in Fontainbleau. Though some very good recent material has also been provided locally by the Champions of Change group, assembled by Sex Discrimination Commissioner Elizabeth Broderick.

American researcher Anna Fels offered a perceptive but confronting analysis of female attitudes, concluding that 'women refuse to claim a central purposeful place in their own stories, eagerly shifting the credit elsewhere and shunning recognition, and without earned affirmation, long-term learning and performance are rarely achieved. Ambitions are both the product of and, later on, the source of affirmation.'[15] In her experience, women didn't identify their ambitions till later in their professional lives, when children had been raised, sexual identity was settled and the 'capacity to manage relationships and do the things described as feminine is no longer in doubt'. Only then, said Fels, did the mastery and resilience required for mature leadership fall within the women's reach.[16]

Creating sufficient leadership motivation among women at that point was the challenge. Landmark studies in 2008 and onwards have made the case that companies with numbers of women in executive, boardroom and leadership positions deliver consistently better returns than those which don't. (They estimate about fifty-eight per cent better over a four-year period.)[17] This is not because the female gender equals profit, but because diversity at higher decision-making levels goes hand in hand with developing firms that are nimble, adaptable and more ready to re-evaluate their systems compared with those with lesser degrees of diversity at the top. In a globalising world, amid an ever-deepening ICT revolution, these vital characteristics tend to be found in companies that cope with threats to their existing business models.

The McKinsey researchers drew up nine yardsticks of good leadership practice that improve organisational performance: participative decision-making, being a role model, offering inspiration or a compelling vision of the future, defining expectations and responsibilities clearly, developing your people, offering intellectual stimulation, communicating efficiently and with charisma, engaging in individualistic decision-making, and emphasising control and then corrective action if necessary. Women applied five of these nine behaviours more frequently than men, the research found. It was the last two where men were considerably ahead of women. This is quite significant and emerges in various studies. Women tend to be extremely consultative and highly engaged with their teams. They are highly focused on enabling their people to adapt, and this represents a big plus. Men achieve those targets less well, but they react to crises in original and decisive ways. They are comfortable with creating some disruption, which can also be a distinct asset in acute circumstances. Men have the 'capacity to bring their people along with them' despite the inevitable turbulence.

Men can be 'egotistical, rule-breakers and upstagers', qualities judged to be extremely important at certain points, according to American researcher Nancy E. Parsons, from the CDR Assessment Group in Tulsa, Oklahoma. She found that women could default to 'worrier' mode when challenges piled up, that they could exhibit fear-of-failure characteristics, which could exhaust those seeking to promote them. The key was to coach the women into not resorting to these self-defeating and self-doubting tendencies.[18] Indeed some women self-sabotage by not knowing when criticism is genuinely constructive and by recoiling from any possiblility of it from a better positioned colleague. In a *Harvard Business Review* blog, Peter Bregman offered some tips for handling 'surprise' criticism: he suggested women look beyond their feelings in order to listen better, that they even look beyond the delivery of the criticism itself. 'Don't agree or disagree, but ask questions. Explore the criticism with a third party whom you trust and, later, decide what you want to do with the information.'[19]

In January 2009, Herminia Ibarra, Robin Ely and Deborah Kolb published an article in the *Harvard Business Review* entitled 'Women and the Vision Thing'. It was based on thousands of wide-ranging assessments from around the world. 'As a group, women outshone men in most of the leadership dimensions measured… including, empowering, energising, designing/aligning, rewarding/feedback, team building, tenacity and emotional intelligence. The exception was envisioning, the ability to recognise new opportunities and trends in the environment and develop a new strategic direction for an enterprise.'[20]

Some crucial pieces of advice emerged from the valuable McKinsey Leadership Project: be aware, the authors warned, about 'second generation gender bias'—that is, inherent and unspoken biases about female leadership. These were subtle and easily missed, akin to 'something in the water', as the researchers said, but they created conditions in which women failed to thrive. So a woman rising happily through the ranks, but blithely unaware of these unseen trip wires, could be brought unstuck easily. They recommended that women wrap themselves and their leadership identity into the core business of the organisation, what the researchers called 'anchoring in purpose'. This moved colleagues past female stereotypes, and towards shared goals and challenges, boosted by the female leaders' strengths.[21] One other suggestion really appealed to me: 'positive reframing'. Women were encouraged to reconsider their reactions to a bad day or experience. Ideally, according to the advice, women should limit their thoughts about the event to a temporary and specific response and keep them impersonal. They should draw up a specific plan to move beyond the decision, act on it—then do something restorative, like meeting friends, going to a concert or indulging in their hobby.[22]

The McKinsey research noted that men tended to build broader, shallower networks in their organisations, whereas women made deeper and narrower connections. Women's relationships in these networks were usually less influential; which meant that women often didn't meet the sponsor deemed so vital in the rise to upper ranks, someone beyond the straight mentor. And, perhaps surprisingly, the Denver-based Forte Foundation, which fosters the next generation of female business leaders in the US, nominated a poor understanding of reciprocity among women as a deficit in their approach. Women 'just didn't get it', or see the need for it, but could definitely be made aware of its importance.[23]

'Ten Traits of Women Business Leaders', compiled by Elissa Sangster from the Forte Foundation, presents the idea of reciprocity thus: 'The term "networking" smacks of good ol' boys and smoky backrooms, but as diversity in business improves, networking is no longer a dirty word. It just means building relationships with colleagues with whom you have something in common—giving, as well as asking for, input and advice from a community of colleagues you cultivate over time.' She quoted material from the Johnson Graduate School of Management at Cornell University in the US, which also found that women need to learn to negotiate better. Women just didn't negotiate as often or as effectively as men, its research group said, due to a complex mix of socialisation, stereotypes and bias, which affected their remuneration and influence.[24] The good news was that these skills could all be learned.

Yes, there are differences between males and females at very senior levels at our current stage of development. But are those differences great enough to warrant *nine times* less advancement to executive ranks, which is the Business Council of Australia's estimate of female versus male progress in Australia as of November 2013? Surely not. Under Elizabeth Broderick's guidance, the Business Council of Australia has nominated some admirable targets designed to break the glacially slow pattern of change in women's participation. BCA members have now agreed they will aim for fifty per cent female directors in executive positions by 2020. For a dose of rare optimism, it's worth reading its excellent 'Increasing the Number of Women in Senior Executive Positions' document, accompanying the launch of the Male Champions of Change network, which comprises twenty-one of Australia's most prominent male CEOs. Far more than anything produced in Australia till now, this research suggests a serious intent by men in power to examine why so few women occupy those senior positions. Under 'style, fit and chemistry', which are commonly cited as reasons not to hire senior females, lead researcher Meredith Hellicar summarised the challenge at hand: 'Given the strength of the "think-leader-think-male" mindset, women—atypical leaders—are often perceived as going against the norms of leadership or femininity.

They run the risk of not having a clear identity in the eyes of others, with their behaviour often being viewed as more like men's by other women, and at the same time either condemned by men for being too stereotypically female, or for behaving in a masculine way (when they exhibit leadership traits prescribed as male). It is important to be aware of the potential for double-bind evaluations, which penalise women both for stereotypical female and male styles. As such, they have a narrower range of behaviours available to them and great expectations placed on them by interviewers and decision-makers.'[25]

Our understanding of why women don't advance more quickly into positions of leadership is improving, as these various sources reveal. The greater focus offered by the last decade of research also limits, I hope, the indignation felt by a lot of women and their supporters when they're blocked by what seems to be caprice or, worse, vindictiveness. Both those elements may be present. And it doesn't make the situation fair. But the detailed body of research does give a constructive overview, in my view, of what the existing workplace prioritises, and points to what might mutually advantage women and productivity. As the research demonstrates, progress will involve far more than merely nominating and grooming women of talent, and then hoping they'll make their way through the ranks to improve conditions for those arriving after them. Individual women, the people who love them and their communities will need to wrestle with how much they genuinely want change at the higher ranks. Only then will more women thrive as our leaders.

A FINAL WORD

'Be yourself. Everyone else is taken.'

OSCAR WILDE

THE nature of ambition has emerged as a vital undercurrent of this book. Ambition seems to be a word heavily freighted with values deemed both desirable and potentially corrupting. Perhaps Australians struggle to find a good definition that fits with our own lives, given that so much of our national tradition has emphasised egalitarianism, with a certain cautiousness about aspiring to rise above the rest. So for women, newly exploring advancement, wariness or even confusion is possibly even more marked. I can't test that empirically, but all my interviews led me towards that conclusion.

None of the women who told me their stories would have arrived in their positions—or to these pages—without ambition, but few of them consciously cited it. I had to glean the role it had played in their lives. Some of the women were distinctly diffident about naming it. And not one nominated anything like the explicit 'reach for the stars' sermon, often preached in modern management manuals, as a prerequisite for success. I think it would have turned them off. So it leaves me thinking about how a woman explicitly stretches herself and expands her range? How much risk needs to be taken with her identity and with others' identities, with those playing supporting roles? There is much discussion of the great juggling act for modern women trying to manage the double shifts of work and home. It is usually described as a time-management issue, but I sense a deeper internal audit, more related to judging one's essential character. Most of the women with children I interviewed were now looking back on those dilemmas, most of their kids having grown up. They chose not to dwell on the sometimes agonising permutations of divvying up their time between professional and private duties, endlessly debating with themselves and their husbands or partners (if they were lucky) about organising the schedule. They are not memories I care to prioritise even though, by and large, I did manage, with a lot of help. But at times, the competing demands were exceptionally challenging, and I'm not sure that our household dealt with it ideally. So I found the ABC's managing director Mark Scott's remarks particularly interesting, about coming to terms with the complexity of his senior female managers' lives. And Telstra's David Thodey's explicit hopes that the working world be a venue for people's best selves. And Ann Sherry' and Wendy McCarthy's convictions about their workplaces fully respecting the bigger dreams of employees, by dignifying them with high quality and regular communication. Until a lot of their peers accept something similar, and adapt their methods, change won't happen.

All people in power, male and female alike, need to grasp the underlying issues outlined by the women in this book: how is the cup of energy in any one life distributed fairly between duty, joy and ambition? It is a profound question, critically important to the workplace and families alike.

Nearly fifteen years ago, I happened upon a conversation that helped me tease out some elements of this debate that I think are worth remembering. As part of Churchill Fellowship research into social cohesion undertaken in London in 2000, I attended a colloquium run by a young Anglican minister, who invited us to consider how the Old Testament had treated ambition. He focused on the book of Genesis and the story of Joseph (popularised in the musical *Joseph and the Amazing Technicolor Dreamcoat* and the animated feature *The Prince of Egypt*), the epic tale of an exceptionally talented young Jewish man who was thrown out of home by jealous brothers, and who rose to become one of the Egyptian Pharoah's most trusted advisors. His success hadn't been Joseph's plan; the Jews, after all, were enslaved in Egypt. But he made choices, the minister suggested, to serve his god by using his talents to accept whatever was asked of him, whether or not he understood the reasons, and to put his talents at the service of others. The yield for Joseph, much to his surprise, was a steady rise through the levels of power and influence within the Egyptian system. Even more, when his elevated position brought him once again into contact with his treacherous brothers, he behaved like Mandela did with his captors: he forgave and forgot and emerged majestic.

Joseph had listened to a powerful inner voice; he had discerned correctly between means and ends and, therefore, used his talents not to climb ladders but for their own sake. What are the implications for us, grappling with ambition 2000 years on?

That an ambition to develop your gifts (or talents), as opposed to your ego, is not only okay but also actively blessed. It amounts to an inspired mix of hope and fatalism, not too far from Hilda Scott's description of relinquishing control. This notion might help tease out some of the contemporary dilemmas people face in approaching their careers.

However, I certainly did not emerge from a year of immersion in this book believing that everyone should aspire to formal leadership, even though I relished meeting people who were seriously enjoying their power and influence. Oh, how I applaud the women I've featured: the way they've climbed their mountains, the risks they've taken, the fun they're having—though not continuously, of course, because their schedules are truly daunting, with little room for impromptu events. But there's an air of abundant life about them and that is inviting. They are game and magnificent—but they are not all of us.

The Danish television series *Borgen*, which I watched during 2012–13, had a big impact on me. Centring on a female prime minister in a minority social democratic coalition government, its brilliant scripts and characterisation brought to vivid life the nature of winning, losing and just scraping through in politics and in family life. It was so real, so plausible. Here was a talented mother aiming super high, a good father unprepared for real gender equity, and children just coping in between, sort of. The toll seemed too great for the gains made, a conclusion I hated drawing. It set me thinking about life cycles and ideal timing and the everyday bravery required of those who break stereotypes—like the women I've met—to take on the powerful jobs. Don't let us imagine it is a casualty-free zone.

The broader leadership discussion within our communities

is pretty intense these days. Naturally, most of us would like to be well led. Everyone yearns to meet a good leader, as one of life's supposed epiphanies. Even more, many of us are encouraged to believe that *we* have a leader within. I sense that many people now believe aspiring to leadership, wherever they sit in the community, ennobles them almost more than any other talent—more than aspiring to be a good parent or a good wife or a good worker in your field.

The ambition for leadership seems to have crept up on us over the last generation. Maybe traditional Downton Abbey–type hierarchies have been so flattened it's simply worth tilting at the leadership windmill. Is it a by-product of emphasising the individual rather than the group? Surely it's now accepted that champion teams, rather than teams of champions, win grand finals. Yet the yearning to be seen as a leader competes with, sometimes even transcends, the desire to be seen as a champion, which is quite revealing of our times.

That great line of Germaine Greer's from way back in the 1970s has never left me: 'When all's said and done, when women finally got the key to the executive washroom, all they discovered inside was the lavatory.' Yet the experience of scrabbling for that key is eulogised as the apex of good citizenry, sometimes as the only challenge that really counts. Oddly enough, through researching this book, I came to the opposite conclusion. Many of us, possibly the majority of us, couldn't and shouldn't consider the sorts of trade-offs that leadership requires. More than ever, I am convinced that a lot of us should aim instead to be Very Good Followers. We should suck that particular lolly for a while, resisting all the clamouring for glory, and see how it tastes, even though it might be a life lived less intensely, which has its consequences too. I rather like that truism about the real risks facing a person who's decided to take no risks in life.

'Most of us have jobs that are too small for our spirits,' wrote Studs Terkel in *Working*, his famous book of the early 1970s. Almost fifty years on, his world of working-class heroes has been pretty much dismantled. Now we are grappling with a new-order labour model that doesn't conform to neat work–home boundaries at all, but invades most corners of our lives. For the sake of our serenity, we need to reclaim free time so we can gaze at the world around us. Doing one's allotted task in life to the best of one's ability—this is a definition of sanctity that I heard years ago from a Perth priest, and I think that sums it all up really. Lead and enjoy doing so, if talent and circumstances beckon. Or thrive on being well led by others. That could be just as much fun.

NOTES

1. Herminia Ibarra, Robin Ely, Deborah Kolb, 'Women Rising: Unseen Barriers', research conducted at INSEAD, Fontainebleau, France, first published *Harvard Business Review*, October 2008, republished *Australian Financial Review BOSS*, October 2013.
2. Interview with author on ABC TV's *Nationwide*, Sydney, March 1983.
3. Boris Groysberg and Katherine Connolly, 'Great Leaders Who Make the Mix Work', *Harvard Business Review*, September 2013.
4. Herminia Ibarra, Robin Ely, Deborah Kolb, 'Women and the Vision Thing', research conducted at INSEAD, Fontainebleau, France, published in *Harvard Business Review*, January 2009, republished in *Australian Financial Review BOSS*, October 2013.
5. Annie Lawson, 'Out of the Hot Seat', *Age*, Melbourne, 8 September 2005.
6. Mihaly Csikszentmihalyi, *Flow: The Psychology of Optimal Experience*, Harper Perennial, New York, 1991.

7. Michael Marmot and Jospeh Siegrist, *Social Inequality in Health: New Evidence and Policy Implications*, OUP, 2006; *Social Determinants of Health*, World Health Organisation, 2008.

8. *Male Champions of Change Report*, Business Council of Australia, Sydney, November 2013.

9. Michelle Grattan, 'Liberals' Second-in-Charge Needs to Lift Her Game and Soon,' *Age*, Melbourne, 5 December 2008.

10. McKinsey Research Team, 'Female Leadership: A Competitive Edge for the Future', Women Matter 2, *McKinsey Quarterly*, New York, 2008.

11. 'Women In Defence', Department of Defence, Canberra, 1 December 2012.

12. Directors Resources Centre, 'Statistics', Australian Institute of Company Directors, Sydney, July 2014.

13. Ibarra, Ely, Kolb, Women Rising: Unseen Barriers', 2013.

14. Hugh Son, 'Wall Street Women Have Gone Backwards', *New York Times*, republished in the *Australian Financial Review*, 2 February 2014.

15. Anna Fels, 'Do Women Lack Ambition?' *Harvard Business Review*, April 2004.

16. *Ibid*

17. George Desvaux, Sandrine Devillard-Hoellinger, Mary Meaney, 'A Business Case for Women', *McKinsey Quarterly*, Vol 4, 2008.

18. Nancy E. Parsons, 'A White Paper', CDR Assessment Group, Tulsa, Oklahoma, 1 May 2013.

19. Fiona Smith, 'Give Yourself a Sporting Chance when You're Criticised', *Australian Financial Review*, 20 November 2013.

20. Ibarra, Ely and Kolb, 'Women and the Vision Thing', 2009.

21. Joanna Barsh, Susie Cranston, Rebecca Craske, 'Centered Leadership: How Talented Women Thrive', *McKinsey Quarterly*, September 2008.

22. *Ibid*

23. Elissa Sangster, 'Ten Traits of Women Business Leaders: It's Not What You Think', *Forbes Magazine*, 8 August 2012.

24. *Ibid*

25. Meredith Hellicar, 'Improving Recruitment, Selection and Retention Practices', Business Council of Australia, Sydney, November 2013.

ACKNOWLEDGMENTS

WHEN I pitched this idea back in July 2013, Text publisher Michael Heyward wisely said this book would be a significant journey for me personally, let alone a worthwhile project, and he was right. It has felt like a marathon, insisting on a much steadier and more durable commitment than is required for my usual media work. It tapped all my demons—procrastination, fear of failure, panic—and tested me at various levels. It is a solitary climb yet you reach the finish line because other people have joined in: a life lesson if ever there was one. So I am especially grateful to all the women who took part, who took a punt on me and trusted that I would represent fairly their precious stories of their dreams, stumbles, falls and triumphs. What a privilege it has been to hear their accounts and convey them to other Australians. I hope the women believe I have done them justice. I hope the men who participated do so too, because in some ways they were stepping into particularly tricky territory. They were generous with their experiences and seemed pleased to be asked.

My primary thanks are to my *Saturday Extra* colleagues at ABC Radio National: executive producer Jackie May and producers Kate MacDonald and Kate Pearcy. They not only encouraged this project, but also tolerated my related stresses and strains and took on extra loads whenever I had to rush off to grab whatever time these super-busy successful women could grant me. This was especially demanding towards the end of 2013, at an exceptionally busy time of the year. Sound engineers Tom Hall, especially, and Steven Tilley were incredibly helpful in rescuing some of my interviews when the recorded sound was compromised. Tom never said no to any request for help, though he must have been tempted to throttle me occasionally when he was very busy with his main duties. His advice on the technicalities of recording and of sourcing the best device were invaluable. The team at ABC-TV *Compass* deserve thanks too. They noticed, I'm sure, but kindly didn't dwell on how my already busy schedule had become that much fuller, making me less available for meetings and voiceovers. The various transcription typists from Pacific Solutions and Phonetype in Brisbane were remarkably efficient and, more than that, delightfully generous and explicit in their enjoyment of the interview material, which really buoyed my morale during those early months when the endgame seemed a depressingly long way off. I appreciate all those who quietly briefed me, whether or not they even realised it, by offering their views over copious coffees, meals, deep-and-meaningfuls, character-building arguments and editorial meetings. Jess Cross, from Soul Gym, listened to my ongoing updates for months, as she put me through my fitness paces.

I offer real gratitude to everyone at Text Publishing, who were so instantly encouraging about my idea that it both thrilled and terrified me. But my editor, Jane Pearson, especially deserves a very big thank you. I think we've learned a lot from each other and from our impressive women. Jane had to accommodate unexpected time demands from my work schedule, like television work in Israel, which added considerably to production pressure, and I deeply appreciate her dedication over all these months.

My dear friends have been stalwarts. They provided their usual nurturing as well as some normalcy throughout the last twelve months: Lyndall Crisp, Graham Fox, Lucy and Stephen Chipkin, Warren Scott, Norman Swan and Karen Carey, Jan and Greg Matthews, Patricia Evans, Mary and Carl Ciccarelli, Christine Shervington and Jan Holdsworth. Leonie and Andrew Condon listened to many of my dilemmas and read early drafts of some chapters. Bonnie Boezeman's extensive knowledge of the arena of executive women, shared over years of watching the Swans together at the SCG, infused my writing and contributed to the whole project. Maxine McKew's experiences of producing a book were a balm. And my old friend Helen Trinca's support was critical, both her copy-tasting at some vital moments and her encouragement. My ABC colleague Dina Volaric helped me research the stories and collated material on female leadership. She also coped admirably with last-minute fact-checking and proofreading, and anticipating my needs. I could not have completed the book without her. My part-time PA Nicole Coghlan alone knows how vital she is to the effective management of my over-committed life. She problem-solves and soothes simultaneously: everyone needs a Nicole.

To my family I offer my most sincere thanks for putting up with me: Genevieve, her husband, Craig, and little Taya, Michael, and especially to my daughter, Eliza, who bolstered unfailingly in her inimitable style when needed, her husband, Adam, and the newest member of the clan, young Sean. In some important ways, they become collateral contributors, as their lives were drawn inexorably into their mother's creative dream. They have generously changed outings, sympathised with my worries and, above all, listened and offered good thoughts when I stalled for one reason or other. But I owe the biggest debt of all to my son Sam, who has lived beside me throughout this yearlong rollercoaster ride. Not only has he helped me meet deadlines, but his technological advice has also been invaluable. All Baby Boomers need a Gen-Y digital native beside them as they create, and he never let me down. What's more, he did so with a smile and apparent genuine concern for his occasionally frazzled mother. I trust that he and his generation enjoy a fairer working world where both his male and female friends' talents for leadership and authority are equally respected.